Chinese Swords

An Ancient Tradition and Modern Training

中
國
劍
客

An Anthology of Articles from the *Journal of Asian Martial Arts*

Edited by Michael A. DeMarco, M.A.

Copyright © 2015 by
Via Media Publishing Company
941 Calle Mejia #822
Santa Fe, NM 87501 USA
E-mail: md@goviamedia.com

All articles in this anthology were originally published in the *Journal of Asian Martial Arts*.
Listed according to the table of contents for this anthology:

Pegg, R. (2011)	Volume 20 Number 2	10 pages
Pegg, R. (2001)	Volume 10 Number 3	12 pages
Yang, Lianto, & Figler (2004)	Volume 13 Number 3	25 pages
Berwick, Hsu, & Dong (2009)	Volume 18 Number 1	20 pages

Book and cover design by Via Media Publishing Company
Edited by Michael A. DeMarco, M.A.

Cover illustration
Lu Junhai evades then attacks Reza Momenan's wrist.
Illustration courtesy of Hon Lee.
www.jowgashaolin.com

ISBN: 978-1-893765-11-5

www.viamediapublishing.com

contents

CHAPTERS

preface

The Chinese double-edged straight sword (*jian*), the "gentleman of weapons," is the focus of this e-book. There are a growing number of people interested in this fascinating weapon, its history, and its use. For your convenience, this anthology assembles the best articles on this subject as published in the *Journal of Asian Martial Arts*.

Chapters 1 and 2 were written by Dr. Richard Pegg, a scholar of Asian studies and art curator with over thirty years of studies in the martial arts. With sound academic and practical experience in swordsmanship, Dr. Pegg writes here on ancient Chinese bronze swords and also on the parallels of Chinese calligraphy and swordplay. The analysis and presentation of the calligraphic illustrations give insight into the physical execution of sword movement. These superb presentations provide a perspective that is useful for understanding the technical and historical significance of the sword arts in China.

In the next chapter, Tony Yang, Andy Lianto, and Robert Figler give an excellent overview of the fundamentals of training with the straight sword. This article outlines some of the most famous sword forms in history, Liu Yunqiao's lineage, solo and two-person practice, as well as details on fundamental techniques and their combinations. For all intents and purposes, the practice and perfection of these fundamentals make one a master of the sword. Over 140 photos are used just in this chapter to illustrate the techniques.

Stephan Berwick's chapter details the history and practice of a famous straight sword system, the Qingping (Green Duckweed). The study meshes Chinese- and English-sourced research and a revealing interview with Lu Junhai—the grandmaster of this unique sword system. The interview is conducted by America's senior Qingping disciples, Reza Momenan and Hon Lee.

If you are a serious practitioner of the Chinese double-edged straight sword and have an interest in its history and techniques, you'll enjoy each chapter included in this anthology. May it be a handy reference work for information as well as a source of inspiration for actual sword practice.

Michael A. DeMarco
Santa Fe, NM
August 2015

author bio notes

Stephan Berwick, M.A., has a Chinese martial arts background spanning over thirty years. Bow Sim Mark was his early mentor. He went on to work for martial arts Hong Kong film director Yuen Wo Ping (*Crouching Tiger, Hidden Dragon* and *The Matrix*). Upon returning to the US, Mr. Berwick began intensive Chen taiji training under the celebrated Chen stylist Ren Guangyi, and also closely mentored by top members of taiji's founding family, the Chens of Chenjiagou. Mr. Berwick holds an M.A. in international law from the Fletcher School of Law and Diplomacy, Tufts University in cooperation with Harvard University. http://truetaichi.com

Robert A. Figler, Ph.D., is an associate professor of management at the University of Akron and teaches courses in human resource management and international business. His area of international specialty is China and he has been involved in Chinese martial arts for over twenty-five years. He is a disciple of Tony Yang and trains primarily in baguazhang, bajiquan/piguazhang, and Chen-style taijiquan.

Chris Hsu, Ph.D., is currently an assistant instructor at the Jow Ga Shaolin Institute, specializing in Yang taijiquan. He also recently worked as a Chinese interpreter, after spending twenty-three years at the Department of Defense as a human resources psychologist. Mr. Hsu holds a Ph.D. in industrial psychology from North Carolina State University.

Hon K. Lee, M.S., M.B.A., and dipl. acupuncture, is director of the Jow Ga Shaolin Institute. He first learned Jow Ga gongfu from Dean Chin and Hoy K. Lee in Washington, DC, and later trained with masters throughout the Far East. He is a Jow Ga disciple under Chan Mancheung, as well as a Mizong and Qingping sword disciple under Lu Junhai. He learned Cha-style weaponry from Chen Enyi, a senior disciple of the late Cha grandmaster Ma Jinbiao. He also practices traditional Chinese medicine and is owner of the Sports Edge Acupuncture Clinic in Herndon, Virginia. Mr. Lee is a former marine officer and foreign affairs specialist, holding an M.S. in national security strategy from the National War College, an M.B.A. from the NY Technical Institute, and a professional diploma in acupuncture.

Andy Lianto is a commercial photographer, filmmaker, and martial arts instructor. He has taken classes in filmmaking at New York University. He has competed nationally and won gold medals in bajiquan, piguazhang, and Praying Mantis, and is a disciple of Tony Yang.

Reza Momenan, Ph.D., is chief instructor of the Jow Ga Shaolin Institute and a founding member and official of the Northern America Chinese Martial Arts Federation. He started his martial arts training in the mid-1970s in Shotokan karate and started Jow Ga training under the supervision of the late Dean Chin in 1979. Mr. Momenan became a disciple of Lu Junhai, studying Mizong and Qingping sword. Mr. Momenan is the founder of the Chinese Boxing Academy at the George Washington University and head of the Chinese Martial Arts Club at the National Institutes of Health (NIH). He holds a Ph.D. in medical engineering and serves as a research scientist at the NIH.

Richard A. Pegg, Ph.D., has a Ph.D. in East Asian art history from Columbia University. During his more than thirty years of martial arts study he has focused on Shotokan karate, aikido, and taijiquan, with an emphasis on swords. He has been studying with Harvey Sober since 1978. Dr. Pegg is currently curator of Asian art for the MacLean Collection in Illinois. His recent publication is *The MacLean Collection: Chinese Ritual Bronzes.*

Tony Yang is the instructor and owner of the Wu Tang Center for Martial Arts in Akron, Ohio. He began his training in traditional Praying Mantis at age six under his Uncle, Wang Shujin, and later became a disciple of Su Yuchang. Su then introduced Tony to Liu Yunqiao and Yang became a disciple, following him on a daily basis for eight years. Tony's primary training is in bajiquan/piguazhang, bagua, Six Harmony Praying Mantis, mizongyi, xingyi, longfist, Yang and Chen taijiquan styles, and numerous weapons.

Ancient Chinese Bronze Swords
in the MacLean Collection

by Richard A. Pegg, Ph.D.

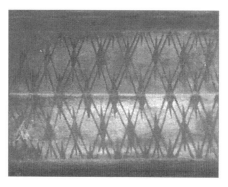

Fig. 1–2: Chinese sword and blade's detail.
Late Spring and Autumn (770–476 BCE) to Early Warring States Periods (475–221 BCE),
bronze, 47 cm, MacLean Collection. *Photograph © Bruce M. White, 2008.*

The MacLean Collection of Asian Art, located near Chicago, is primarily housed in a building completed in 2004 and designed by architect Larry Booth of Chicago. The Asian art collection consists of perhaps 55 percent Chinese objects and 40 percent Southeast Asian objects, with the remainder being from other parts of Asia. The collection is focused on three media: pottery, bronze, and stone. The ambition behind the collection has been to seek unique examples, the best that can be displayed and investigated, thus ultimately contributing to the knowledge about these objects and the peoples who used them.

One of the great strengths of the MacLean Collection is the quantity and range of its ancient bronze objects, including drums, bells, weapons, and vessels from China and Southeast Asia. Bronze is a copper-based alloy that includes lead and tin. The casting process of northern and central China, as used in the famous Houma foundries in modern Shanxi Province, utilized the piece-mold method since the thirteenth century BCE. The ancient bronze weapons in the MacLean Collection include a range of swords, knives, daggers, halberds, spearheads, arrowheads, and crossbow triggers.

In ancient China, swords (*jian*) were weapons typically with a long, straight blade, sharp edged on both sides, with one end pointed and the other fixed in a hilt or handle. This sword (figure 1), dating from the Late Spring and Autumn (770–476 BCE) to Early Warring States periods (475–221 BCE), is 47 centimeters in length. With a grayish-brown patina, it consists of a blade and an integrally cast hilt. The blade is straight from the hilt to the midpoint, while the remaining half of the blade is slightly curved and tapered to the tip. The shape of this weapon is designed specifically for close fighting, using the forward edges to cut or slice. The blade is still extremely sharp, and the slight curve of the forward half of the blade is designed for maximum cutting effect, as the blade is pushed toward or drawn back across an opponent. The thick wing-shaped guard slightly exceeds the width of the blade and is decorated with an abstract zoomorphic mask of turquoise inlay. This inlay design was likely an emblem specific to the rank of the person who carried it. The hilt shaft is rhombic in shape, with two ring rolls designed to hold the girt in place. The hilt terminates with a hollowed, domed pommel that is decorated using concentric rings on the exterior. The two seam lines on the hilt correspond to the two edges of the blade, confirming that this weapon was cast using a two-piece mold.

The blade is decorated with a menacing, now-darkened, barbed rhombic or diamond pattern, resembling the appearance of modern-day razor wire (figure 2). The production of this type of decoration requires special technical skill, so weapons with this decoration are considered rare. It is said that swords with this decoration were crafted by the master hand of Ouyezi in the ancient state of Wu. After scientific testing, scholars posit that the decoration was achieved by modifying the rich tin delta phase used in hardening the sword's blade. The high-tin layer of this phase enabled finer sharpening and the holding of the sharpened edge. Here, a more complex process involving a mix of tin, iron, and silicon was also skillfully laid onto the blade to achieve this effect (Chase & Frankin, 1979).

The typological study of Chinese bronze swords is still not mature. Lin Shoujin has generalized three types of bronze swords according to hilt shapes: flat hilt without pommel and guard; hollow or half-hollow cylindrical hilt with narrow guard and round, tray-shaped pommel; and solid cylindrical hilt with wide guard and round, tray-shaped pommel (Lin, 1959: 75). This sword belongs to the third type—a type prevalent in the middle and lower Yangzi Valley of central China. Earlier forms of this type of sword have also been found in the south of China, leading some scholars to argue that their origin is from that area (Li, 1982: 47).

The overall length and the proportion of length to width are important criteria in dating Chinese swords. They are derived from bronze daggers, with the blades continuously lengthening over time. By the end of the Warring States period, swords became so long that they became impractical. Sixteen of the seventeen swords found in the first pit of the terracotta army beside the mausoleum of the first emperor Qin Shi Huang (259 BC–210 BC) are around 90 centimeters long (Zhong, 1996: 182–3). If using the lengthening of the sword for dating, this 47 centimeter-long sword should be an early example. In considering some other Late Spring and Autumn period examples (Wang, 1993, no. 80, and Zhongguo Kexue, 1959, fig. 67.7), which are longer than this piece but very similar in shape, we date this sword to the Late Spring and Autumn to Early Warring States periods.

The next sword, dated to the Middle Warring States period, is 66.5 centimeters in length (figure 3). The blade of this sword, similar to the previous sword, is almost straight for roughly half of its length before narrowing to a tapered tip. On the narrowing half, the two edges curve slightly inward, again a design for cutting or slicing in close-quarters fighting. The cross section of the blade is an elongated octagon consisting of four wide body facets and four narrow edge facets. The plain narrow guard is a flattened diamond in shape. The hilt is a combination of the tang of the blade, which inserts into a U-shaped prong that gradually expands to the disk pommel. A small round rivet hole is provided for binding the two parts of the hilt together. The pommel is flat and hollow in the center. The blade and the hilt are grayish yellow, though the hilt is covered by a thin, dark gray layer, likely caused by the deteriorated grip bindings. The blade is decorated with a similar menacing, but worn, barbed rhombic or diamond pattern, resembling the appearance of razor wire, similar to the pattern found on the previous sword.

Fig. 3: Chinese Sword
Middle Warring States Period (475–221 BCE), bronze, 66.5 cm, MacLean Collection.
Photograph © Bruce M. White, 2008.

This sword (figure 3) belongs to the type with a flat hilt, which appeared in the Late Spring and Autumn period, and has been broadly found in many places (Lin, 1962: 75–80). The addition of the round back hilt is very rare. In most cases, the flat hilt was inserted into a wooden handle (Gao, 1959: 31), with the remains of wooden handles having been found in many places (Luoyang, 1959: 97). The addition of the round back hilt can be seen on several swords. A 75.6 centimeter-long example from Changsha city, Hunan Province, was dated to the Middle Warring States period (Hunan, 2000: 465, 604). The present sword is slightly shorter than the Changsha example, and longer than the Late Spring and Autumn examples, so we date it to the Middle Warring States period, while considering the possibility that it may be from the Early Warring States period to the Early Western Han dynasty (206–9 BCE).

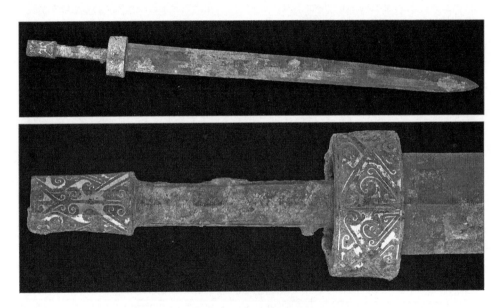

Figs. 4 and 5: Chinese Sword and detail
Warring States Period (475–221 BCE), bronze, 63.7 cm, MacLean Collection.
Photograph © Bruce M. White, 2008.

A sword dating to the Warring States period is 63.7 centimeters long (figure 4). It is unusual, as the blade and hilt were integrally cast. The overall proportions and cross section of the blade are very similar to those of the previous example. Here, the blade is slightly bent to one side, probably the result of an old repair, midway down the blade, and another more recent repair closer to the tip. Also, the shape of the lower half of the blade does not have the slight inward curve found on other swords in this collection. Like the previous sword, the cross section of the blade is an elongated octagon consisting of four wide body facets and four narrow edge facets. The wide body facets have a slight pitting to their surface, while the edge facets are polished smooth. The flat hilt slightly narrows toward the pommel and matches the octagonal cross section of the blade. The long pommel, with a slight taper toward its end, continues the octagonal cross section motif in a more rounded, evenly faceted manner. The thick, wide guard is hollow, and its cross section is oval. Remains of the wooden grips are still found in the hollow space inside the guard and around the hilt. Evidence of fine textile is also found inside the guard and covering two-fifths of the guard, indicating that this sword was wrapped in textile when interred in a tomb.

The wide guard and elongated pommel create an ideal location for the elegant abstract geometric patterns in gold and silver (figure 5). No other swords have been found that match this particular example. In comparison to the previous sword, its similarities, including the blade length and octagonal cross-section designs, lead us to date it no earlier than the Early Warring States period.

Fig. 6 Chinese sword
Western Han Dynasty (206–9 BCE), bronze, 45.7 cm, MacLean Collection.
Photograph © Bruce M. White, 2008.

Another sword, dated to the Western Han dynasty, is 45.7 centimeters in length (figure 6). The proportions and shape of this sword are very similar to those of the first sword, and it was probably based on a similar blade. The blades are the same length and width; however, this blade has a flatter profile, unhardened edges, and a less menacing appearance. The construction of the hilts is the same for both, with the rhombic hilt shaft with two ring rolls and domed pommel all designed to hold the girt in place. The hilt on this sword is more than a centimeter shorter, the guard is flatter and not inlayed, and the exterior of the pommel is smooth. The two seam lines on the hilt correspond to the two edges of the blade, confirming that this weapon was cast with two molds. In comparison with the first example, this sword appears to be more ceremonial than functional, as the unsharpened, uneven, and broken edges of the blade suggest.

The blade, guard, and pommel are gilded with gold, while the perimeter of the blade, hilt shaft, and pommel exterior are not. The gilded body of the blade is engraved with an elongated dragon design. Near the guard are two dragon heads facing outward on the two sides of the median ridge. Their eyes, mouths, and horns are all clearly presented, while their elongated bodies are composed of a complex abstracted design. The dragon's two tails merge, forming a point, perhaps a phoenix head, at the tip of the blade.

Though this sword is very similar to the first in shape, its decoration leads us to date it to the Western Han dynasty. The technique of gilding on bronze can be traced back to the Early Warring States period, and some small gilded bronzes have been found in Warring States tombs. However, the technique developed significantly during the Western Han dynasty (Zhu, 1995: 557) and began to be applied on vessels and larger objects. Gilded swords have not been well reported, so the gilding alone cannot provide useful information on dating, but its smaller size leads us to date this sword to the Western Han dynasty.

In ancient China, knives (dao) are weapons, regardless of their length, that are sharp edged on one side only, with the other side typically thick and blunt. The dao is one of the most popular weapons in ancient China. This type of knife probably originated from the sword. Such an evolutionary relationship can be inferred by comparing the shapes and uses of the sword and knife. The structural differences between a knife and a sword are that the guard disappears and the tip is much less sharp. These are tactical differences. The sword was designed for close fighting with cutting and stabbing. The knife was used only to cut and developed in response to the increased use of cavalry, since a galloping cavalryman makes many more cuts than stabs (Sun, 1991: 134).

Fig. 7, Chinese Knife
Western Han Dynasty (206–9 BCE), bronze, 81.3 cm, MacLean Collection.
Photograph © Bruce M. White, 2008.

This knife, dated to the Western Han dynasty, is 81.3 centimeters in length (figure 7). This weapon consists of a long, narrow blade with an integrally cast hilt without a guard. The length of the blade in profile can be divided into fifths—

one-fifth for the handle, three-fifths for the body, and one-fifth for the tip. The blade too can be divided into fifths—three-fifths for the slightly narrowing body and two-fifths for the beveled edge itself.

The blade has a very slight taper to the tip, which curves gently, ending in a sharp curve and rather blunt tip. The flat continuous back of the hilt through the tip is straight. At the pommel the thickness is eleven millimeters, and at the tip the thickness is five millimeters, making for a substantial weapon. The hilt is squared, top and bottom, with a trapezoidal cross section. The oval pommel is circular in cross section and cast into the hilt.

Fig. 8, Chinese Knife Detail
Western Han Dynasty (206–9 BCE), bronze, 45.7 cm, MacLean Collection.
Photograph ©Bruce M. White, 2008.

Diagonal parallel vestiges on the hilt confirm the wrap pattern of the grip (figure 8). The oval pommel is gilded in gold. The design of its front section, also the end of the hilt, has an X pattern inside a rectangle with clouds in mushroom forms, like the Chinese ceremonial scepter (*ruyi*) patterns. The rest of the pommel is decorated in a pattern of scrolling clouds.

Similar bronze knives have been found in tombs at Shaogou village, near Luoyang, Henan Province. The blades on those knives are much thinner and thus were probably used for ritual, not battle. The ring pommel is overwhelmingly found on all Han dynasty (206 BCE–220 CE) knives, with a great variety of designs (*Luoyang*, 183 and Sun Ji, 134). This type of knife developed in the Western Han dynasty and, based on the generalization that bronze weapons were thoroughly replaced by iron weapons at the end of the Western Han dynasty, we can date this knife to that period (Yang, 2002: 123).

These five weapons are representative examples of the more than forty ancient Chinese bronze swords and knives found in the MacLean Collection.

References

Hunan Provincial Museum, et al., (2000). *Changsha chumu* (Chu tombs in Changsha). Beijing: Wenwu Publishing Company.

Chase, W., and Frankin, V. (1979). Early Chinese black mirrors and pattern-etched weapons. *Ars Orientalis*, 11: 215–58.

Gao, Ming (1959). Jianguo yilai Shang Zhou qingtongqi de faxian yu yanjiu (Discoveries and study of Shang and Zhou bronzes from the State of Jian). *Wenwu*, 10: 24–31, 36.

Li, Boqian (1982). Zhongyuan diqu Dongzhou tongjian yuanyuan shitan (Explorations of sources of Eastern Zhou bronze swords of the central plains). *Wenwu*, 1: 44–8.

Lin, Shoujin (1962). Dongzhou shi tongjian chulun (Early discussions of Eastern Zhou bronze swords). *Kaogu xuebao*, (2): 75–84.

Luoyang Shaogou Hanmu (Han tombs at Shaogou in Luoyang) (1959). Beijing: Kexue Chubanshi (Scientific Publishing Company).

Sun, Ji (1991). *Handai wuzhi wenhua ziliao tushuo (Explanations of Han Dynasty material culture)*. Beijing: Wenwu Publishing Company.

Wang, Zhenhua (1993). *Guyuege cang Shang Zhou qingtong bingqi*, (Shang and Zhou bronze weaponry: C. H. Wang Collection). Taibei: Guyuege.

Yang, Hong (2002). Handai bingqi erlun (Han Dynasty weapons: Two discussions). In *Yifen ji: Zhang Zhenglang xiansheng jiushi huadan jinian wenji (Festschrift for Zhang Zhenglang's 90th birthday)*. Beijing: Shehui Kexue Wenxian Chubanshe (Social Sciences Documentation Publishing House), 115–23.

Zhong, Shaoyi (1996). Gudai tongjian de changdu jiqi yiyi. In Wang Zhenghua, *Shang Zhou qingtong bingqi ji Fucai jian tezhan lunwenji* (A collection of essays relating to the "Shang and Chou bronze weaponry and sword of Fuchai exhibition"). Taibei: Guyuege, 181–6.

Zhongguo kexueyuan kaogu yanjiusuo (Academica Sinica Archaeological Research Institute) (1959). *Luoyang Zhongzhou* (Zhongzhou Road, Luoyang). Beijing: Kexue Chubanshi (Scientific Publishing Company).

Zhu, Fenghan (1995). *Gudai Zhongguo qingtong qi (Ancient Chinese bronze utensils)*. Tianjin: Nankai Daxue Chubanshe (Nankai University Publishing House).

Chinese Sword & Brush Masters of the Tang Dynasty (618–906)

by Richard A. Pegg, Ph.D.

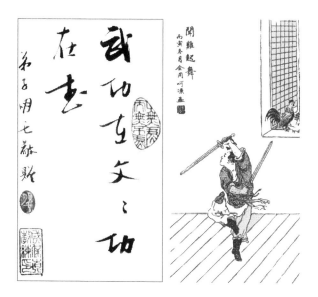

"One's martial achievements lie in the cultural and one's cultural achievements lie in the martial."

Album leaf, ink on paper. *H. I. Sober Collection.*

Figure at right, from "At cockcrow I begin to [sword] dance."

This essay briefly introduces several of the close relationships that existed between the wielding of the sword and the wielding of the brush during China's Tang dynasty.[1] I juxtapose terminology from both forms of artistic expression and discuss several aspects and fundamental principles of calligraphy that often are overlooked and not focused upon either by art historians or martial artists. As shall be seen, the similarities in training and visual manifestation of these arts are very closely aligned and are as vital today as they were a thousand years ago. Several historical anecdotes that clearly demonstrate the associations between sword and brush masters from China's past also are explored.

Calligraphy, considered the highest form of expression in the visual arts of China, can be appreciated on many levels. Fundamentally, it can be viewed as words because each character signifies a meaning. That meaning can be elevated through the medium of a poem of correct rhyme and meter that conveys sense through content and form. At another equally important level, calligraphy represents a visual, aesthetic expression of brushwork that creates rhythms and relationships of space.

Figure 1: *Spiritual Flight Sutra.*
attributed to Zhong Shaojing, ca. 738.
Calligraphy courtesy of The Metropolitan Museum of Art, Purchase, The Dillon Fund Gift, 1989. (1989.141.1 e).

The *Spiritual Flight Sutra*, attributed to Zhong Shaojing (active ca. 713–741), and now in the collection of the Metropolitan Museum of Art, is a good place to begin (fig. 1). This essentially Daoist text was originally commissioned in 738 by the princess Yuzhen, daughter of Tang dynasty emperor Xuanzong (847–860).[2] The present focus is on the calligraphy of the text itself. In terms of form, each stroke of the brush is traditionally observed for itself and how it relates to connecting strokes when combined in a specific order that composes each character and, in turn, each line of prose or poetry. The structure of every character is, in fact, said to imitate the human body and some of the fundamental aspects of nature (fig. 2, left). We speak of the bones, flesh, and sinews of each character and the stabbing, hooking, and slashing of the brushwork, all terms that obviously apply to a sword master as well as to swordplay itself. It can be seen that each character is physically balanced and harmonious. Like the posture of a master swordsman, the posture of a character requires a natural balance. It can be seen that in calligraphy every stroke, hook, and dot is perfectly executed, demonstrating clean crisp movements done both with graceful and sharp turns. The swordplayer too must demonstrate strong, smooth, and sharp strokes for each sequential posture in a form. There is also the reading or flow of one character into another like one posture into another. In other words, both for calligraphy and swordplay, the descriptive terminology utilized applies equally.

Figure 2

Yang-style taiji broadsword forms juxtaposed with
six characters from the *Spiritual Flight Sutra.*

If it is remembered that calligraphy is the presentation of forms in a particular time and space, it is then a kind of performance art. The written characters are the visible traces that the brush has taken over the path of the paper or silk. In Chinese calligraphy, in the same way that one is able to follow every movement of a master and his sword, it is understood that the viewer is able to recreate every trace of the movement of the brush and mentally follow the actual process of creation in all of its consecutive phases. One has the sense of actually watching the calligrapher perform in front of one's own eyes. Using a brush in this manner in the medium of ink on paper reveals every nuance of the calligrapher. The calligrapher cannot return and touch up mistakes because they would immediately be recognized as such. This of course implies an understanding of the process involved in being able to recreate the moment of creation, but it also means that the viewer is able to establish an immediate rapport with the artist. It is said that there is a direct dialogue; one can actually understand what the artist was thinking and feeling and see into his personality.

When calligraphy is viewed as a kind of performance art, the relationships of time are understood in the actual movements of the artist's brush, sometimes reckless then careful, swift then slow, or blunt and wet then thin and dry. Spatial relationships are created that cause tension between the characters as they relate to each other, one after another. There are rhythms in single characters and in vertical lines of characters, as well as rhythms between one line of characters and the next. In figure 2, a string of six successive characters (detail from fig. 1) is juxtaposed with six diagrams from a Yang-style taiji broadsword form.[3] Notice the similarities between the postures and movements of the brushwork of the six characters in the line of calligraphy and the swordwork of the six sequential postures of the form. Uniformity of style is apparent within each character or posture as well as from one character or posture to another in both visual presentations. Each character of calligraphy presents a different stance and posture in a continuous sequence, from tall to squat or from static to everything moving simultaneously. The swordplayer too moves high and low or comes to rest and then moves every limb simultaneously. Here again the calligrapher's brushwork, with its variety of sword cuts and strokes, presents a myriad of solutions to the problems of brush, ink, paper, space, and time in composition. In similar ways, the swordsman presents his solutions to the problems of sword, space, and time. It is interesting to note that the actual size of each written character is less than 1/4 of an inch and yet, as has been seen, the strength of the presentation is equal to that of the full human body.

Masters of sword and brush often state that the sword or the brush moves of its own accord. To achieve that state, *qi*, the intrinsic energy that permeates the entire universe, is drawn into the body. There is focus and concentration; qi then flows out of the tip of the sword or brush as guided by *yi*, intent of mind. The cut and movement of blade or brush must be smooth with no mistake. A

viewer can follow the traces of the tip of the brush or watch the tip of the sword. The sword can actually appear to "move" from one end or the other, i.e., from the tip or from the handle. For example, in Yang-style taiji the sword often moves from the tip and in Wu-style taiji the sword moves from the handle. This gives the appearance that in Yang style the sword moves around the body whereas in Wu style the body moves around the sword.

Figure 3
"At cockcrow I begin to [sword] dance."

12

The seamless and effortless demonstration of brush or sword is achieved through daily practice and devotion to one's art. As we know, the extensive training required results in what might be called disciplined spontaneity. Here, the scene of "at cockcrow I begin to [sword] dance" (*wenji qiwu*) depicts the swordsman's devotion to daily practice (fig. 3).[4] Ongoing and continuous practice to achieve and maintain mastery is essential. This practice begins and ultimately ends with the simple daily repetition of basic strokes and movements. Only with constant practice is the master able to effortlessly perform and unconsciously create an expression that is uniquely his own.

For calligraphy, the basic training methods have been outlined in the well-known text *Battle Plan for the Brush* (*Bizhen tu*), often translated as *A Diagram of the Battle Formation of the Brush*, attributed to Madame Wei (Wei Furen, 272–349).[5] Madame Wei is considered to have been the teacher of Wang Xizhi (ca. 303–361), the great calligrapher who developed new forms of cursive and running scripts and transformed calligraphy into a new means of personal expression. *Battle Plan for the Brush* is, however, most likely a work of the Tang dynasty (618–906).[6] The interplay of the terms *wen* (literary accomplishments, civil, culture, or elegant and refined) and *wu* (military or martial) define each other in this work.[7]

The text begins with an introduction, a description of the best materials to be used for calligraphy, including brush, inkstones, ink, and paper and a list of proper techniques for holding the brush to achieve different calligraphic styles. At one point the text reads "When writing dots, verticals, horizontals, slices, waves, hooks, and curves all must be sent off with the full strength of one's body." This could just as easily apply to sword techniques. Eventually, a list of seven stroke types is presented (fig. 4):

1) *Horizontal stroke*: Like a cloud array stretching a thousand *li* [Chinese miles], indistinct, but not without form.

2) *Dot stroke*: Like a stone falling from a high peak, bouncing and crashing, about to shatter.

3) *Left down stroke*: The tusk of an elephant [thrust into and] breaking the ground.

4) *Oblique hook stroke*: Fired from a three thousand pound crossbow.

5) *Vertical stroke*: A withered vine, ten thousand years old.

6) *Right down stroke*: Crashing waves or rolling thunder.

7) *Horizontal with fold and hook stroke*: The sinews and joints of a mighty bow.

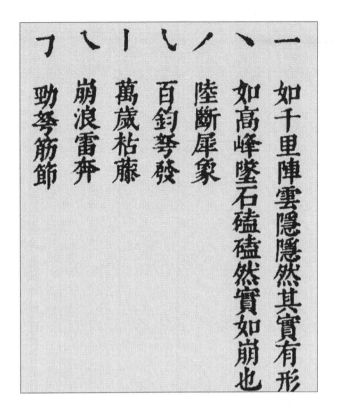

Figure 4

Battle Plan for the Brush, detail. Attributed to Madame Wei (272–349).

In a rather simplistic and fundamental way, these seven strokes, as visual forms, can be paired very nicely with single postures in a sword form, such as those found in the double-edged straight sword form of Shaolin Six Harmony Gate style boxing.[8] The horizontal stroke can be paired with a transitional posture of a movement called "turn body, split and chop" or *fanshen piduo* (fig. 5). Notice at the far right the presence of the same small hook created with the hand for one and ink for the other. The dot stroke can be paired with a portion of a posture called "open the window and view the moon" or *tuichuang wangyue* (fig. 6). The left down stroke can be paired with the final transitional posture of "turn body, split and chop" (fig. 7). The oblique hook stroke can be paired with a transitional posture of a movement called "withdraw step and gather blade" or *chebu gouna* (fig. 8). The vertical stroke can be paired with the first posture and opening stance called "stand erect and lift elbow" or *zhili tizhou* (fig. 9). The right down stroke can be paired with a posture called "pull up weeds and search for snakes" or *bacao xunshe* (fig. 10). The horizontal stroke with fold and hook can be paired with a transitional posture of a movement called "three rings cover the moon" or *sanhuan taoyue* (fig. 11). The visual parallels are striking between the seven essential brush strokes as defined in *Battle Plan of the Brush* and the seven body positions from the sword form presented here.

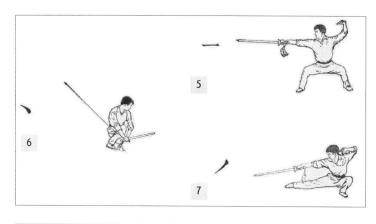

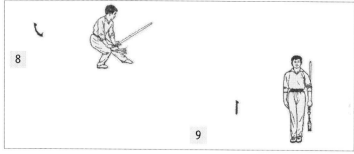

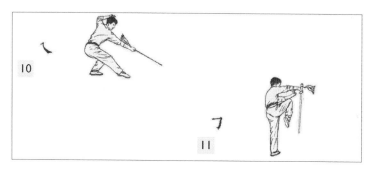

Figures 5–11

Shaolin Six Harmony Gate (*liuhemen*) straight-sword form, details.

Battle Plan for the Brush continues: "The seven strokes above represent a plan of the battle array of the brush, charging in and pulling back, slashing and chopping. There are seven manners of wielding the brush." Again, this is a description that could just as easily represent sword techniques. The text continues: "Those who hold the brush far back and yet work with speed, and those in whom [and once again here is that term used in sword practice as well] the intent, *yi*, precedes and the brush follows, will be victorious." This type of description reminds us of *Master Sun's Art of War* (*Sunzi bingfa*), especially in the final line of the "Terrain" (*dixing*) chapter: "Know the enemy and know yourself; your victory will be without loss. Know the heavens [weather] and know the terrain; your victory will be total."[9] *Art of War*, perhaps the most famous text on military strategy, was written some eight hundred years earlier than and seems to be a very likely model for the descriptions in *Battle Plan for the Brush*. Both texts present a set of guidelines to be followed, practiced, and executed to achieve the same goal: victory.

There are numerous recorded anecdotes describing the relationships between great swordsmen and outstanding calligraphers, painters, and poets during the Tang dynasty. Perhaps the best-known "performance art" cursive calligraphers are the progenitors of wild cursive calligraphy, Zhang Xu (fl. ca. 700–750) and Huai Su (725–785). Huai Su, in his only extant genuine work, the handscroll entitled "Autobiography" (zixu tie, 777) in the National Palace Museum in Taipei, presents a magnificent example of the wild cursive calligraphy (*kuangcao*) as a bravura performance.[10] Both Huai Su and Zhang Xu were known to drink heavily and, when facing a large screen or wall, they would write bold free-flowing calligraphy in an explosion of activity, filling the entire writing surface. But it is Zhang Xu who is credited as the first great performance art calligrapher. His exploits with famous painters and swordsmen are legendary.

In the late ninth century it was recorded that:

> General Pei Min offered Wu Daozi (painter active ca. 710–760) a commission in return for a mural painting commemorating the general's parents. Wu refused the offer and said to the general: "I have heard of your great art of swordsmanship. If you perform for me, it will inspire me, and in return I shall paint the mural for you." General Pei gave a spectacular performance of the martial sword. Wu Daozi then picked up his brush and [in a short time] dashed off a mural. Zhang Xu was present and added his calligraphy. All those present exclaimed that the "three wonders" had marked a special day.[11]

Here the significance and close relationship between the Tang dynasty's most famous sword master and two renowned brush masters are considered together on equal terms.

Another anecdote records: "As an artist Zhang Xu was a bohemian and lived entirely according to his mood. He loved wine and did his best work under its influence. While listening to the music of a street band and watching a sword dance by the courtesan Gongsun, he discovered the secret of pace and rhythm." Figure 12 is a late nineteenth century woodblock print depicting Gongsun performing with double straight swords.[12] The passage continues "From daily occurrences such as this, he learned structural relationships in calligraphy. [Tang dynasty] Emperor Wenzong (reigned 827–840) considered Li Po's (705–762) poetry, General Pei Min's swordsmanship, and Zhang Xu's wild cursive calligraphy the three perfections of the Tang dynasty."[13] In this anecdote, the Tang emperor equates and recognizes the close relationship between *wen* and *wu*, the cultural and the martial. There can be no question that martial and calligraphic prowess were considered to be equal in importance during this period.

Figure 12

Madame Gongsun
Performing Sword Dance.

Even the famous Tang dynasty poet Du Fu (712–770) wrote a poem, entitled "On Seeing the Sword Dance of a Pupil of Madame Gongsun," that speaks of Zhang Xu calligraphy and this famous lady's sword dance. The prose preface sets the stage:

During the second year of the Da Li period (768), in the tenth month, on the nineteenth day, at the home of Yuan Zhi, the Administrative Aide in Kiuzhou, I saw the girl Li the Twelfth from Linying do a sword dance. There was strength and elegance in her movement. I asked her who was her teacher, and she said: "I am Gongsun Daniang's disciple." In the third year of the Kai Yuan period (716), when I was just a lad, I remember being in Yancheng and seeing Miss Gongsun do an entire sword dance [see fig. 12]. In the beginning of Emperor Xuanzong's reign, of the two imperial court schools Spring Court and Pear Garden, it was made known that only one dancer was considered the finest by the emperor, that was Gongsun. Ahhh, her beautiful face and elegant clothing faded as my white hairs grew. Now too her disciple is no longer young. I see that the styles of master and student cannot be distinguished. Cherishing the moment I am inspired to compose a Sword Dance Poem. Once Zhang Xu from Wu, who was known for cursive calligraphy, saw, while in Ye prefecture, Gongsun dance the West River Sword Dance. Afterward his cursive calligraphy greatly improved, showing martial and magnificent qualities for which he was grateful to Gongsun![14]

This preface is followed by the poem. This short passage describes not only the intradisciplinary master-student relationship with the sword, but also an interdisciplinary relationship between sword and brush. Zhang Xu the calligraphy master was inspired to improve his own calligraphic style by watching Gongsun perform with the sword. The stories associated with Zhang Xu learning by watching the sword typify the ongoing interaction of wen and wu at the time. They demonstrate that the similarities in training and visual manifestation of these arts are very closely aligned.

In closing, Chinese calligraphy exists as a two-dimensional record of the performance of the calligrapher, the master of the brush. In the same way, diagrams or photographs can be a record of the performance of the master of the sword. In either case, the mind of the viewer has the opportunity to actively participate in the action of the brush or the sword. Both formats imply a narrative because there is a progression through the image space that is physical as well as visual and intellectual. As we have briefly seen, a text describing cursive calligraphy could quite easily be used to describe sword play and vice versa. There is a well-known martial arts expression that in typical

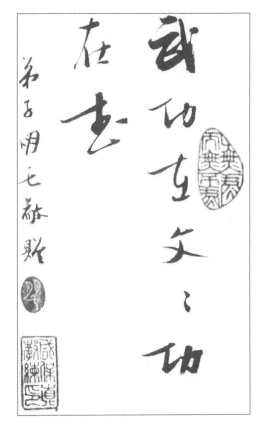

Figure 13

18

Chinese fashion plays with the terms for culture and military, *wen* and *wu* (fig. 13). Recently written in a very sharp and angular calligraphic style, like sword cuts, the text is composed of two parallel lines of four characters each, for a total of eight characters, that reads *wugong zai wen; wengong zai wu* or "one's martial achievements lie in the cultural and one's cultural achievements lie in the martial." Like the logo for the *Journal of Asian Martial Arts*, which joins pen and sword in a single image, these anecdotes, examples of calligraphy, and the *Battle Plan for the Brush* demonstrate well the interaction between sword masters and brush masters as well as the concepts of wen and wu. The principles and practices in calligraphy and sword play from China's Tang dynasty not only transcend time but relate to all culture in China, whether literature and painting or Shaolin martial arts, and are as vital today as they were a thousand years ago.

Notes

[1] The author thanks the Chinese Military History Society for organizing the panel at which a version of this essay was first presented during the Association of Asian Studies annual meeting in San Diego, California, March 2000.

[2] For more on *The Spiritual Flight Sutra* (*Lingfei jing*) see Qi Gong, "Qi lingfei jing sishi san hang ben" (On the Forty-three Columns from the Spiritual Flight Sutra), *Yiyuan doying*, 1987, no. 34.

[3] Based on figures found in *New Approach: Chinese Kung-fu Training Methods*, Commercial Press, Hong Kong, 1984. See pp. 97–137 for entire form and explanations.

[4] See *Zhongguo huapu dazidian* (Dictionary of Chinese Painting), Taiwan reprint, 1968, *Gujin renwu huapu*, p. 15.

[5] For a brief biography of Wei Furen see Zhang Yanyuan, *Fashu yaolu* (Essential Record of Calligraphy Exemplars), Taiwan reprint, ch. 8, p. 129.

[6] See Barnhart, Richard M. "Wei Fu-jen's Pi Chen T'u and Early Texts on Calligraphy." In *Archives of Chinese Art*, XVIII, 1964, pp. 13–25.

[7] The complimentary terms *wen* and *wu* are often juxtaposed to demonstrate the necessity for balance between the civil and the military. The logo for the *Journal of Asian Martial Arts* demonstrates this by joining the stylus of a pen with the blade of a sword to represent a harmonious whole.

[8] For entire form with explanations see *Shaolin liuhemen* (Six Harmony Gate Boxing of Shaolin), Fujian chubanshe, 1984, pp. 134–164.

[9] See *Sunzi bingfa*, ch. 10, p. 24 in *Zhongguo bingshu jicheng* (Complete Collected

Military Texts of China), Shenyang, 1987. For English translation see Griffith, Samuel B. *Sun Tzu The Art of War*, Oxford University Press, 1963.

[10] See *Ku-kung shu-hua lu* (The National Palace Museum Catalogue of Painting and Calligraphy), Taipei: National Palace Museum, 1956, vol. 1, ch. 1.

[11] See Zhu Jingxuan, *Tangchao minghualu* (Famous Paintings of the Tang Dynasty), reprinted in *Wangshi shuhuaduan* (Wang's Garden of Calligraphy and Painting), ed. Wang Shih-cheng, 1589. Reprinted Shanghai, 1922, Vol. 6, pp 1–3. See a different version of this story in Guo Ruoxi, *Tuhua jianwenzhi*, ch. 5, p. 69; see reprint *Huashi congshi*, Shanghai, 1963.

[12] See *Zhongguo huapu dazidian* (Dictionary of Chinese Painting), Taiwan reprint, 1968, *Meiren baitai huapu*, second half of collection, p. 27.

[13] See *Tang Shu* (History of the Tang Dynasty), ch. 202, lie zhuan 127, Wen-i II, Li Po and Zhang Xu, p. 9.

[14] For preface and poem see *Quan tangshi* (Complete Tang Poetry), ch. 222, p. 2356.

Basic Chinese Sword Training and Practice

by Tony Yang, Robert A. Figler, Ph.D.,
and Andy Lianto

Tony Yang practicing with the double-edge sword in Anchorage, Alaska.
All photos courtesy of Tony Yang. Photography by Andy Lianto.

Introduction

It has often been said by traditional Chinese weapons practitioners that it takes three years of training for the staff and single-edge sword and ten years of refined training for the spear and double-edge sword (*jian*). Although not to be taken literally, it does point to the amount of time and training necessary to achieve a high level of proficiency in the spear and double-edge sword practice. Regardless of the degree of skill refinement, all of these traditional Chinese weapons, including the elite Chinese double-edge sword, require a strong foundation in basic training exercises.

The focus of this article is on basic training in the traditional Chinese sword methods of Liu Yunqiao as transmitted to Tony Yang.[1] It should be noted that there exists no authoritative treatise on basic double-edge sword training and it should *not* be assumed that the methodology illustrated in this article is the last and final word on the subject: This is only one of the many ways to attain skill and proficiency in the Chinese double-edged sword.

Historical Watermarks

From kings to generals, poets to priests, the Chinese sword has served to both kill and inspire. For war, exercise, pleasure, entertainment, and ceremonial symbolism, the sword has done it all over the span of centuries. A weapon of antiquity, the sword finds its beginnings in the 16th and 17th century BCE (Kang, 1995: 21) and has achieved global renown through the popular movie, *Crouching Tiger, Hidden Dragon* and in many of the worldwide sword performance competitions. In 496 BCE, during the reign of the Wu and Yue, the sword also proved to be an equal opportunity employer. A female sword master called Yue Nu was employed by the king to train his soldiers. Yue Nu's methodology equated open-hand forms with swordplay and provided the following guidelines:

> The combination of position, breathing, and consciousness; harmony of the internal and the external; offense and defense; and both static and moving states [from *Spring and Autumn Annals* of Wu and Yue]. —Kang, 1995: 26

In the Later Han Dynasty (25–200 CE), sword dancing and the ritualistic wearing of the sword became popular with the Emperor and among court officials. Han sword stone carvings from the 184 to 220 CE were excavated in Zhengzhou, depicting sword fencing and sword against spear practice. During the Warring State period swordplay also served as entertainment (Kang, 1995: 29–39) which continues today as standardized routines in performance competition throughout China and the world. Although the historical citations and variant approaches are almost endless (see Table I for a partial list of some of the famous sword series), the art of the sword can be roughly grouped into three broad category categories.

TABLE I   Famous Martial Arts Sword Series

1) Hun Wu (Brother)
2) Qingping (Green Duckweed)
3) Qi Xing (Seven Star)
4) Taiji (Grand Ultimate Polarity)
5) Wudang (Wudang Mountain)
6) Da Mo (monk Bodhidharma)
7) Ba Gua (8 Trigram)
8) Ba Xian (Eight Immortals)
9) Pure Yang (Masculine)
10) Lian Huan (Linking Chain)
11) San Cai (Three Parts: hand-body-feet)

12) Hui Long (Winding Dragon)
13) Long Xin (Dragon Form)
14) Long Xing (Dragon Travel)
15) Ci Hu (Stab the Tiger)
16) Bai Yuan (White Ape)
17) Yue Nu (Southeast China Girl)
18) Jing Hong (Shock the Rainbow)
19) Luan Pi (Random Chop)
20) Kun Lun (Kun Mountain)

See Note 2 for additional references.

The first category is the **sword as dance**. The choreographed routines are presented more or less as a dance, often accompanied by music. The postures and strikes are for entertainment only and serve the audiences well. In this category little sword skill is exhibited and there is not much to be absorbed. Sword dance is as popular now as it has been in ancient China, and along with the fan, is now often performed as part of festival/ceremonial demonstrations by retirees in the mainland.

The second broad category is **sword as sport**. Here the sword practice serves primarily as exercise and aids in the individual mobility, stretching of limbs and overall flexibility. This type of practice does not require substantial training but does, on occasion, require the development of average to good sword skill. However, practitioners still treat it simply as sport and exercise. There are few, if any, actual applications to be learned.

The last category, the **sword as martial art**, is the least currently known but the most important for readers of this chapter. Here much of the sword method lies in the systematic training of the wrists. Postures and steps must be effectively coordinated for offensive and defensive moves. Every posture must be practiced over and over again. Open-hand skill acquired at the basic training level is often a prerequisite for this type of training and the swordplay assumes a substantial degree of correct body alignment, structure, and power. The body, mind, and sword of the practitioner must meld into one. The traditional methods are dangerous, surprising, and deadly. It is said that the practitioner must be as still as the "young virgin and quick as a rabbit." A veil of mysticism may arise from the mists of Wudang Mountain (home of many sword related tales) but the reality is that the eloquence, grace, and deadliness of the swordplay is born, nurtured, and endured in the valley of the basics. Without basic training, there is no ascent to the mystical realm of sword mastery: There are no shortcuts or secret breathing exercises and meditations that can transform the ordinary into the extra-ordinary.

The Background of Liu Yunqiao's Basic Sword Training

Liu Yunqiao's basic training traces its transmission from warlord General Zhang Xiangwu, who purportedly was trained by the Governor of Hebei, warlord General Li Jinglin and swordmaster Song Weiyi.[2] Li Jinglin was an extremely skilled and generous swordsman. His sword technique is described as embodying the primary characteristics of the Yang taiji sword and is described by Yang Chengfu disciple, Chen Weiming, in the following:

> Yang Chengfu taught me taijiquan and the sword.... Taijiquan postures are the foundation for the sword postures. If there are sword postures that are not from taijiquan postures, I do not know them.
>
> I heard of General Li Fangchen (Li Jinglin), who was skilled at the art of the sword, which he had studied with an extraordinary man. Sun Lutang praised him. This year the general was passing through Shanghai, and I went to meet him. He was extremely refined and capable and generously taught me his method of sword fencing. I found that he completely used the *yao* and legs. This method was not any different from that of taijiquan and the "listening energy" of push hand, only that sometimes, the swords [separated] slightly by perhaps a mere half inch. This is truly the method of the Wudang.
>
> Yang Chengfu never taught a specific set of sword fencing. When this [fencing ability] is attained, the sword form and its application are complete. After I practice it further and become proficient in it, I will write another book to present to the public. —Davis, 2000: 16-17

General Li Jinglin, in turn, learned many of his sword skills from the Daoist sword master, Song Weiyi. Song was initially hired to instruct the officers of Li Jinglin. One of the officers at that time was Zhang Xiangwu, Liu Yunqiao's older "martial art brother" and sword instructor.

> In 1922, while garrisoning the Jinzhou area [of Liaoning Province] one of his officers, Ding Qirui, became acquainted with a martial arts expert Song Weiyi. Song was skilled in baguazhang and the art of the sword, and had written a work [on the sword] in three parts entitled *Wudang Jian Pu* [*Wudang Sword Manual*]. Because of this, Li went to visit him at his residence, and he implored Song to demonstrate with a performance of his sword art. Later, he also invited Song as a guest to his residence in Tianjin, treating him as a distinguished visitor, requesting of Song that he teach him his barehanded boxing method and sword art. Studying with him were Li

Jinglin's officers Jiang Xingshan, Quo Qifeng, Ding Qirui, and Zhang Xian (Zhang Xiangwu). At that time, the sword art of Song Weiyi mainly made use of solo practice and free-form practice (*san lian*). After Li Jinglin obtained this art, he expended great effort, performing extensive research [on this art], and, on the basis of the foundation of solo practice, he also created [six] two-person training sets [*dui lian tao lu*]. Because of this he enjoyed a reputation in martial arts circles for his superb sword technique.

—Chen Style, 1994: 21–22

With regard to Liu's training, Zhang Xiangwu taught him two basic double-edge sword forms: the Kunwu sword and the taiji sword. However, as noted above, great emphasis was placed upon solo practice (single postures, fixed step and moving steps, linked combinations) and two-person combination application/training exercises. In Liu's teaching, as transmitted by Tony Yang, the first and fundamental requirement is to train and develop the sword wrist without regard to form.

Solo Practice and Two-Person Executions

Prior to teaching the principles of the double-edge sword, it is often assumed or required that the student has spent substantial time in intensive open-hand basic training, including stance training for proper alignment and structure. Liu's system of martial arts training requires systematic and structured development of the waist, arms and legs. The sword training takes it further with attention given to the wrist, shoulder, shoulder/elbow, waist, hip and foot. This initial training of sword technique begins with a very simple but profound movement: *jiao*.

Jiao is translated as "to entangle." The basic starting point is illustrated in Figure A1-1 to A1-8 with particular emphasis upon correct wrist, arm, shoulder, and waist development. The sword tip begins with a counter-clockwise rotation while the hand holding the sword rotating in a counter-clockwise direction. One can think of a see-saw whose ends rotate in a circle but whose middle remains fixed. In the same manner, the rotation requires that the middle of the sword remain fixed and the movement is primarily centered in the wrist and shoulder. After a number of repetitions, the direction is changed to clockwise. This exercise must be performed daily and over a long period in order to bring both strength and flexibility to wrists, hands, arms, and shoulders. If done with a properly weighted double-edge sword, it will subtly work flexibility and movement into the waist area and condition the body for the effective transfer of power from the legs. From this point, one may add a partner in a fixed step position. This provides the practitioner with some timing and sensitivity to the movements of the opponent. This is illustrated in Figure A2-1 to A2-8.

The next step in training is to take the *jiao* exercise into a moving step exercise. Figures A3-1 to A3-9 illustrates this well. The two training partners begin their *jiao* movement and also start to walk in a circle. If done properly this forces the practitioner to utilize the waist, shoulder, shoulder/elbow, hip and foot. As one advances in training, this circle walking, like bagua's "soft hand" (*rou shou*), permits the partners to execute numerous offensive and defensive movements. These exercises represent the most fundamental training in the sword work of Liu and must be done repeatedly before any sword form is introduced.

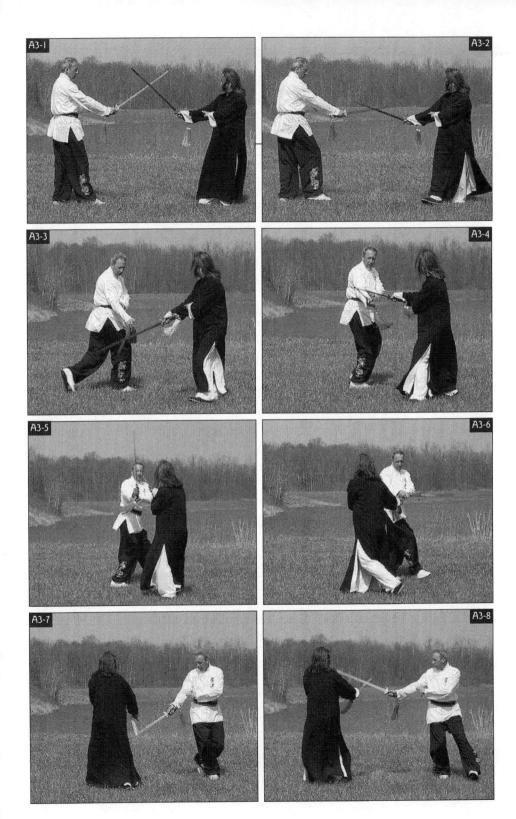

From here, in moving to a deeper level of practice, one must employ the exercises of what is called the *Ten Characteristics Transmission* (Table II). It would be easy to insert the word "secret" and add the mystery of Wudang Mountain to make these principles sound paranormal and spiritual, but such is not the case. This list represents the fundamental essence and applied movement of the skillful sword hand. In progressing from *jiao*, one can execute many of the *Ten Characteristics Transmission* movement out of both fixed step and moving step. Some are done in isolation, some in combinations of two, three or four principles. The exercises embody both offensive and defensive movements and can be executed during the two-person circle walking which adds greatly to full body movement and transfer of power.

TABLE II: Ten Character Transmission

劈 1) Chop (*pi*): sword body moves downward

刺 2) Pierce (*ci*): sword tip moves forward

提 3) Pick up (*ti*): sword handle pointing upward/sword pointing downward

撩 4) Hold up (*liao*): sword tip and blade side point, upward with a backward wrist

抹 5) Wipe (*mo*): sword moves horizontally from left to right

削 6) Whittle (*xiao*): sword body moves diagonally downward

揮 7) Wield (*hui*): sword body moves upward

掛 8) Scrape (*gua*): sword body moves horizontally over the head

弸 9) Stretch (*beng*): sword handle in lower position, sword tip stands vertically upward

錯 10) File (*cuo*): sword tip twists and pierces

B1-1-10: illustrates the solo entangle, dot/point with sword tip (*jiao dian*) movement.

B2-1-8: a two-person fixed step *jiao dian* is shown in this series.

B3-1-8: this series takes the B2 series one step further, showing that the exercise can be done from fixed stance to fixed stance with no circle walking.

B4-1-8: scrape, entangle, dot/point with sword tip (*gua jiao dian*) show a simple combination of some of the *Ten Characteristic Transmission*.

B5-1-8: scrape, entangle, wipe, pierce (*gua jiao mo ci*) show a more complex execution than shown in the B4 series.

C1-1-10: further combinations of the *Ten Characteristic Transmission* are illustrated by the following sequence of stretch and pierce (*beng ci*).

C2-1-8: combinations of the *Ten Characteristic Transmission* are illustrated by the following simple application (*beng ci*).

C3-1-7: combinations of the *Ten Characteristic Transmission* are illustrated by the following complex application of point striking (*beng ci*).

D1-1-10: combinations of the *Ten Characteristic Transmission* are illustrated by the following waist-focused solo practice of whittle and wield (*xiao hui*).

D2-1-9: combinations of the *Ten Characteristic Transmission* are illustrated by the following simple application (*xiao hui*).

D3-1-8: *Ten Characteristic Transmission* combinations are illustrated by the following series of pierce, entangle, whittle, and wield (*ci jiao xiao hui*).

D4-1-9: combinations of the *Ten Characteristic Transmission* are illustrated by the following sequence of scrape, entangle, and wield (*gua jiao hui*).

E1-1-7: combinations of the *Ten Characteristic Transmission* are illustrated by the following solo practice sequence of pick up and hold up (*ti liao*).

EI-6

EI-7

It becomes self-evident that there are a multitude of combinations and two-person applications of the *Ten Characteristic Transmission*. However, this represents a more or less unrefined phase of the sword development and is incomplete. The double-edge sword and its practice must move to a more refined level of skill and usage. Such a level requires the melding of internal and external movement and can be best elucidated by incorporating the principle of Six Harmonies.

Six Harmonies and the Upper Reaches of Swordplay

The Six Harmonies consist of three internal principles and three external principles which are integrated to produce a state where the sword and body move as one. This is primarily accomplished through the slow, intentional, breath co-ordinated play of the sword form. The desired outcome is to produce movement that coordinates and integrates the body, breath, and spirit (*shen*). The three internal harmonies consist of the heart (*xin*) and mind (*yi*), mind (*yi*) and energy (*qi*), energy (*qi*) and strength/power (*li*). These must eventually, be integrated with the external harmonies of eyes and sword, sword and body, and body and steps. This phase of development is time intensive (years) and must be practiced in a relaxed, calm, no release of power (*fajin*) manner.

For the external harmonies one must train for quick eyes, quick sword, and quick stepping. Four directions (left, right, front and back) coupled with upper, middle and lower levels must be closely considered while practicing. However, the inside, or internal harmonies must be well developed in order to find effective and efficient expression in the quick external movements. It is said that the sword master must soar as the dragon, crouch as a tiger, leap as an ape, coil as a snake, and rest as a turtle.

The culmination of the skilled sword practice is said to foster a state of inner- or self-cultivation where the sword movement embodies the spirit, mind and strength/power. The body is said to be flexible and consistent with a focus on the sword to release its spirit. A lifetime pursuit and infinite ascent, many believe that the mastery of the sword represents one of the greatest achievements in Chinese culture. However, all of this presupposes the existence of a raw and unrefined pool of strength/power. Even the most advanced steel making process of the most refined technology requires the input of the highest grade of iron ore to produce the strongest bars of steel. In this sense, the **sword as martial art** can have no "beginners": it only takes the skilled who have already developed the capacity for power generation and expression.

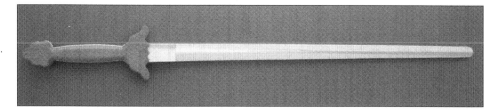

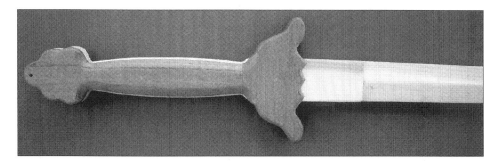

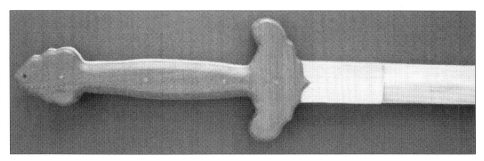

Details of Chinese double-edge swordhandles custom made from Jatoba wood.
The blades are made of hickory. *Photos courtesy of Raven Studios.*
www.little-raven.com

Strength and Power Generation

In some traditional circles, after basic training in stance work and open-hand forms, usually a year or longer, a properly weighted broadsword (*dao*) is introduced into the practice in order to develop full body, semi-refined strength and power. This is normally done by repeatedly executing single moving postures. The weight of the broadsword must be balanced and heavy enough to build external strength and coordinated body movement and yet not so heavy so as to produce unbalanced body strength development. The primary areas most affected by this practice are the arm, shoulder, back area, waist, and grip strength. For example, if done properly, the traditional flower movement of the broadsword will train the waist to direct the upper body movements.

Within that first year, the basic training methods of the staff along with forms and two-person fighting are also taught to add further refinement to the strength and power acquired from the broadsword training. After roughly three years of daily training, it is said that a practitioner will have developed a relatively efficient, strong, well-conditioned body and an acceptable level of fighting skill (this assumes two-person training has also occurred during this time period). In some schools, new material stops here and it is thought that this level of attainment is most appropriate for lower levels of military and personnel.

But there is a different twist for power generation in the training of the baji/pigua practitioners of the Liu Yunqiao lineage. Their bias or favor lies with the utilization of big spear practices, both solo and two-person, from the inception of open-hand training. This training, over the years, is said to develop many internal energies and coordinates them in full body usage along with high levels of strength and power. The exact methods have been elaborated in a previous article (Yang, et al., 2003: 66–79).

In many ways the spear and the sword symbolize the great *yang* and small *yin* and historically it has not been unusual to draw from the principles of big spear training. Ji Jike (1620–1680) took spear theory as boxing theory and created the Mind and Concept Six Harmony Fist (*Xin Yi Liu He*) system which emphasized harmony between mind and body, mind and will, will and breathing, and breathing and strength, hands, and feet (Kang, 1995: 65). In a similar vein, baji master Li Shuwen developed his version of the baji double-edge sword.

Baji Sword: Double-Edge Sword and Big Spear Integrated

Li Shuwen (1864–1934) of Hebei Province, known as "God Spear Li" and bajiquan/piguazhang master, was a strong advocate of continuous big spear (*da qiang*) practice. Some of his famous students were employed in the services of Jiang Jieshi, Mao Zedong, and the last emperor, Pu Yi. Li believed that full-body utilization in the martial arts and high levels of power development could most effectively be brought about by employing twelve (including two-person practice) exercises of the big spear. As Guo (2001) has noted:

> The importance of the lance (*da qiang*) training in the baji system does not limit itself to only destructive power. Of equal importance is its enhancement to the training of empty hand skills and other types of short weapons such as sword fencing.
>
> The power from the leg and waist and the "*kua*" are transferred to the tip of the lance through the arms. This training integrates the body with the lance (*da qiang*) and also can produce, if done properly, a very strong "silk-reeling" force.

As conveyed to Tony Yang by Liu, the creation of General Li Shuwen's baji sword occurred in the Shandong Province around the early 1930s. Li Shuwen, baji disciple Zhang Xiangwu, and Liu were stationed together and Zhang was instructing Liu in the art of the Kunwu sword and its basic training exercises (as illustrated in this article). At one point Li observed the slow, graceful movements of the Kunwu sword form and asserted that it could be made substantially more effective by incorporating power expression (*fajing*) and stomping (full utilization of body weight) at key postures and striking positions. To develop this power in the swordplay of the Kunwu sword, Li observed that many of the big spear movements and their characteristic energies (*jing*) should first be incorporated into the solo practices of the sword and trained as single or multi-linked moving postures. Li then took these movements, in combination with the *Ten Characteristic Transmission* and the twelve or so big spear exercises, and integrated them back into the original Kunwu sword form. The final version of his baji sword embodied the slow, graceful Kunwu movements punctuated by the explosive expression of power and energies of the big spear.

Tony Yang practicing with the double-edge sword in Anchorage, Alaska.

Today, this level of sword play is taught by Tony Yang but is reserved primarily for those students who have trained extensively in the basics of bajiquan, big spear training, and had many years of initial practice in the slow graceful, deep movements of the Kunwu sword. This type of training produces a relatively unique level of sword skill and power that embodies the distinctive imprint of baji's basic training methods.

Concluding Remarks

What has been illustrated in this chapter is one of perhaps many effective approaches in the development of traditional Chinese swordplay and martial arts skill. As one might observe, this line of training is systematic and complete, and designed to extend and deepen the skills of a practitioner who has already been immersed, if not soaked, in the basic training methods of a traditional open-hand system.

There can be little doubt that this time-intensive, physically demanding practice, if done properly, will result in a well-conditioned, self-cultivated practitioner with "inner strengths." But hidden deceptively behind a veil of graceful performance and shroud of mysticism is a deadly art that has served the past emperors and generals of China quite well. It is hoped that other masters of the traditional sword art will bring forth, to the public forum, their training methods, philosophies, and practices for the purpose of preserving and passing on one of China's most long enduring gifts to the world, the art of the skilled sword.

Notes

[1] There are a number of good references now available. One of the most comprehensive sources focused on the Yang Family taiji double-edge sword is: Rodell, S. (2003). *Chinese swordsmanship: The family taiji jian tradition*, Annandale, VA: SevenStars Books and Videos; also see the website for Sword Forum International, http://www.swordforum.com/ and Thomas Chen's listings of Chinese sword resources. Other sources available are: Kobayashi, P. & Kobayashi, T. (2003). *Classical tai chi sword*, Boston: Tuttle Publishing; Olson, S. (1999). *T'ai chi thirteen sword: A sword master's manual*, Burbank, CA: Multi-Media Books; Yang, J. (2000). *Northern Shaolin sword: Forms, techniques, and applications*, Boston: YMAA Publications; Yang, J. (2002). *Taiji sword: Classical Yang style*, Boston: YMAA Publications; and Zhang, Y. (1999). *The art of Chinese swordsmanship: The manual of taiji jian*, New York: Weatherhill Inc.

[2] The basic training exercises presented in this chapter are based on Liu's instruction in the Kunwu sword and taiji sword provided by his senior martial arts brother, General Zhang Xiangwu. Song Weiyi originally instructed Zhang Xiangwu and Li Jinglin (Li Fengchen). It was said that the Kunwu sword and Qingping sword have the same origins and the Kunwu sword may have been a refinement of the Qingping sword. Zhang Xiangwu provided Liu Yunqiao with a Kunwu sword manual but it was lost during the war with Japan. Interestingly, prior to the Kunwu sword, there existed no Wudang sword and some believe that the Yang taiji sword appeared at the same time the Wudang sword was being formulated. Some of these comparisions and sources are cited in the *Kunwu Sword Manual*, Liu Yunqiao, Taipei, Taiwan (Chinese).

Bibliography

Kang, G. (1995). *The spring and autumn of Chinese martial arts: 5000 years*. Santa Cruz, CA: Plum Publishing.

Chen, W. (2000). *Taiji sword and other writings*. (B. Davis, Trans.). Berkeley, CA: North Atlantic Books.

Guo, J. (2001). Spear. www.bajimen.com

The Chen Style Taijiquan Research Association of Hawaii, (1994). Notes on the taiji sword, *The Journal of the Chen Style Taijiquan Research Association of Hawaii*, 2(2), 15–23.

Yang, T., Figler, R., and Lianto, A. (2003). Fajing: Issuing power as practiced in Bajiquan and northern Chinese martial arts systems, *Journal of Asian Martial* –79.

Acknowledgments

The authors wish to express their most sincere gratitude to Ms. Joy Qiu for her translation of the notes taken by Tony Yang in the 1970s on Liu Yunqiao's sword methods. Ms. Qiu is a graduate of Fudan University and a professional translator. She is an active practitioner of Jiang Rongqiao bagua and Yang-style taijiquan.

The authors would also like to thank Mr. James Finley for his appearance in the pictures of the article. Mr. Finley has been a disciple of Tony Yang for over twenty years and is the only student of Tony Yang certified to provide instruction in the bajiquan/ piguazhang system. Also a special thanks to Andy Lianto for his commentary and chapter photographs.

Qingping Straight Sword:
The Last Remaining
Chinese Sword System?

by Stephan Berwick, M.A.
Translations by Chris Hsu, Ph.D., and Dong Xunyin

Zhengduo, leaping in a Qingping sword routine,
mid-1960s. *All photos courtesy of Lu Junhai
except where specified.*

Introduction

China's sword culture remains highly idealized, but as a complete martial art is rarely if ever in evidence today. Traditional Chinese swordsmanship can perhaps be viewed as a martial discipline on the verge of extinction. While contemporary Chinese martial arts teach sword, Chinese swordsmanship today is generally based on a practitioner's specialization on a single sword routine contained in an overall martial system. Elements of Chinese swordsmanship survive with individual forms that, while inspire, appear incomplete.

Today's individual straight sword routines that bear the characteristics of an overall martial system are where traditional Chinese swordsmanship is ensconced. But is there more than this? Do complete sword systems underlie China's ancient, well-documented, albeit rarely seen sword culture? The answer lies in the art of the Green Water Lily straight sword (*Qingping jian*)—a rare straight sword system that survived in the hands of a few and preserves uncommonly rich levels of technique, concepts, and sword ethos representative of classical Chinese swordsmanship—all in a stand-alone comprehensive system suggestive of ancient Chinese sword methods.

Chinese Swordsmanship: Systems vs. Forms

Chinese sword systems, in contrast to individual sword forms, appear to be a missing link in the history of Chinese swordsmanship. The straight sword had not been used as a battlefield weapon since the Jin dynasty (265–420 CE) and as a result, many ancient swordsmanship skills have been lost, but the use of the straight sword as a self-defense weapon was later revived during late Ming (1368–1644 CE) and early Qing Dynasties (1644–1911 CE) (Jones, 2005). So while the Ming and Qing dynasties are considered a Golden Age for martial arts in China, the variety of straight sword forms that emanate from overall martial systems greatly outnumber stand-alone sword systems. Today, this is still evident—straight sword skill is overwhelmingly limited to practice of single routines that are part of a martial art schools curriculum. The prevalence of surviving forms over systems may lie in the societal and political trends of the time.

> Although Ming aesthetes had quite a bit to say about swords as an art form, there is however, little evidence to show that this appreciation remained strong during the Qing. A possible explanation could be that the tastes of China's cultural elite tended to narrow as the centuries passed, becoming ever more preoccupied with arcane details of a few, beloved major art forms such as painting, porcelain, and jade. A parallel can be drawn with the decline of the furniture tradition during the later Qing. Finally, we must also take note of the influence of Confucian values, which tended to denigrate things military in favor of literary interests. During the transition to Manchu rule it may also have been a pragmatic choice for scholars not to show too great an interest in arms. —Tom, 1998

Perhaps China's maturity as a cultural outpost spurred less emphasis on martial arts beyond direct military use. The classic late Ming encyclopedia, *Wubeizhi*, gives bladed weapons relatively scant attention. Despite the fact that edged weapons were a mainstay in the empire's arsenals. It could be that sword technology was so well established by those whose job it was to master it, that it hardly warranted books on the technology (Tom, 1998). Also, the dominance of non-martial artist Confucian scholars—who were vastly more educated than most martial artists—may also explain why few accurate martial tomes were historically produced during China's imperial history (Kennedy & Guo, 2005: 35), a history rife with martial arts development. From an environment where scholarship was dominated by civilians, the more philosophical aspects of martial arts, especially straight sword practice, began to take hold in the civilian population.

> The jian has come to stand for justice, chivalry, integrity, nobility, purity, gentleness, and wisdom. Because it is also considered to be a sacred and magical talisman capable of exorcising evil, the jian has historically been used in religious ceremonies and has been commemorated in legends, poems and songs. Some even regard the jian as a lover, devoting their lives to its practice. Traditionally, the jian is always called *bao jian* (precious sword) and its practice is one of five special disciplines believed to build character through the development of moral integrity, nobility of mind, emotional sensitivity, and physical well being. —Robinson, 2006b

It appears that as the distinct philosophical ideal of the straight sword emerged, written technical manuals dedicated to or inclusive of straight sword technique were not widely produced, as compared to other Chinese martial disciplines. But with evidence of early writings on bladed weapons, the political climate before the collapse of China's dynastic period suggests attempts were made to de-emphasize the promotion of martial arts. The ruling Manchu minority whom formed China's last dynasty (Qing) are often blamed for suppressing all writing on military subjects out of fear of insurgency by the Han Chinese majority.

> The paucity of reference material has not always been the case in China. A survey of technical and artistic treatises reveals a considerable number of works dealing with steel bladed swords, published as early as the 4th century [CE]. (There is an equally impressive body of material dealing with earlier bronze weapons). However, the publication of such works dwindled sharply after the fall of the Ming Dynasty in 1644. It is not known for certain why there is a relative scarcity of reference material written on swords during the Qing, the last imperial dynasty, which fell in 1911. What is interesting, however, about the military books published during the Qing is that they invariably deal with firearms, artillery, and explosive weapons. These texts date primarily from the mid-19th century when the empire was racked by rebellion. —Tom, 1998

However, the most technically dense individual sword forms of various Chinese martial arts appear to be rooted in technical requirements and training indicative of more systematic training, as evidenced in Qingping sword and perhaps other known records of stand-alone sword systems. During the Ming dynasty, a book entitled *Record of Arms*, published in the latter years of the dynasty, features double-hand sword work that is not tied to any specific (overall) martial system. It was simply a collection of techniques that the military author/compiler found to be useful on the battlefield (Kennedy, 2007). Also of note is the famed General Qi Jiguang's manual, the highly influential *32 Canons of Boxing*, published in the mid-1500s, which included General Qi's preferred armed and unarmed techniques drawn from popular martial systems of his day.

During the more recent Republican era (1911–1949), a variety of martial art books were published, largely based on much earlier works (Kennedy & Guo, 2005: 115). As literacy spread, amidst a movement to leverage martial arts for health and self-defense, many martial artists produced books that still hold much influence. But accurate scholarship on sword arts were still rare. One exception is a work by Huang Yuanxiou and Li Jinglin, entitled *The Main Points of Wudang Sword*. Although referred to as Wudang sword, the set was a creation of Li and had no connection to a preexisting, overall martial system (Kennedy, 2007). Thus like much of the best of traditional art forms, deep straight sword knowledge was known to exist, but was transmitted unevenly with dubious sourcing.

The Cultural Revolution (1966–1969) that crippled Chinese society during the 1960s is also to blame for the dearth of records on sword systems. This period compelled the youth to attack all that was considered old and bourgeois, to ostensibly build a new China unencumbered by outdated traditions, superstitions, and any knowledge, art, or discipline that spoke to the old ways. From this rationale, China's Communist government embarked on a social and cultural cleansing that caused the widespread destruction of ancient books, records, and artifacts, while also attacking the people that upheld traditional knowledge and culture. Martial artists were among those targets. As such, the Cultural Revolution caused the destruction of martial art books, records, and ancient weapons, forcing the traditional martial arts community to retreat underground and rely on the oral transmission of their arts. When China began to recover from the turmoil, the government rehabilitated martial arts as a tool for health and well-being, which followed the lead taken by China's first Republican government in promoting and standardizing traditional martial arts. This second effort successfully upheld martial arts as one of the first ancient traditions to be revived and championed in modern China.

Qingping Sword System Rediscovered

From the post-Cultural Revolution revival of martial arts in China, the government undertook an unprecedented effort to conduct field research on traditional martial arts nationally. The effort involved sending out teams of researchers tasked with uncovering ancient martial systems, forms, and weapons to be recorded for posterity as treasured cultural relics and to open access to martial art knowledge. From this historical effort, Qingping sword system was uncovered in present-day Shanghai, the site of important Republican Era martial art development and preservation.

Lu Zhengduo, 1962.

Three generations of the Lu Family, 1976.

In 1983, the excavation of China's martial arts heritage was launched across the country under the National Commission for Physical Culture. The martial art excavation and organization team at the Shanghai Physical Education Academy was tasked to work on recovering and recording the Qingping sword system, based on knowledge about Lu Junhai and his father Lu Zhenduo—Shanghai based grandmasters and heirs of the original Mizong boxing style and the Qingping sword system. Lu Zhenduo's widespread reputation for high-level straight sword technique and famed success as a full-contact fighter in bouts taking place on raised fighting platforms (*leitai*), brought the researchers to his 4th child and inheritor of the Qingping and Mizong ("Lost Track") sword systems, his son Junhai. Upon convincing the younger Lu, whose father had died earlier, that the sword system his father passed to him would best survive if recorded, the researchers studied and recorded the complete system. The team received high reviews at the National Martial Art Excavation and Organization Exchange Conference held in Chengde city, Hebei, in May of 1984, resulting in the production of an extremely rare, now out-of-print book and a non-commercial video record of the routines, from which this article draws.

Lu Zhengduo performing Qingping
style sword in the early 1960s (left)
and in the late 1960s (right).

History of Qingping Sword

Qingping sword was derived from ancient sword practice which was, for centuries, a hidden system. Until publication of a book on the fundamentals of the system in 1930, it was passed just rarely. Originally Qingping sword was the name of an ancient type of straight sword, known for the supreme quality of its blade.

The ancients often gave elegant and uncommon names to those treasured swords with outstanding quality so that they could be distinctive from ordinary swords. In the article written by Chen Lin, it said, "The Monarch Hou Tigao was a rather ordinary talent who relied on the Qingping, an ancient double-edged sword called *Gan Jian*." Chen Lin was a person in the Eastern Han dynasty [25–220 CE], thus, it suggested that the Qingping sword existed in the Han dynasty [206 BCE–220 CE]. Its reputation was not lower than other legendary swords, such as *Gan Jian* and *Mo Xie*. Li Bai of the Tang dynasty [618–907 CE] stated in a letter to Han Jingzhou, "Numerous Qingping were related, and their value grew in the households of Xue and Bian." The Qingping sword mentioned by Chen and Li referred to high quality famous swords. According to the legend, the Qingping sword could slice gold and jade and cut hair. It was unparalleled in its sharpness. The Qingping sword system uses this name, which signifies sharpness and an ability to sweep away all obstacles. —Lu, Qiu, & Wang, 1989: 1-2

The system has been passed on since the mid-1800s, first in Shandong province, then transferring to boxers in Hebei Province. According to a hand-copied book from 1856, the creator of the distinct Qingping sword system was a Daoist monk, Pan Zhenren, who lived at the Dragon and Tiger Mountain, Jiangxi province, whose Daoist name was Yuan Kui (Lu, Qiu, & Wang, 1989: 1–2). Pan Zhenren allegedly meditated, practiced martial arts, and studied literature on the mountain and sometimes would enter the outside world to teach martial arts. From this legend, and as evidenced in the uncommon technical richness of the system, it is believed that the Qingping system was researched in depth, fusing the strengths of many martial art schools, while leveraging Daoist and martial theories, forming a uniquely complete sword system.

Pan Zhenren first taught Daoist monk Meng Jiaohua of Yishui County in Shandong. Meng taught it to another Daoist monk, Feng Xiyang of Lingyi County, Jinan Prefecture in Shandong. Feng then taught it to Yang Kunshan of Haifeng County, Wuding Prefecture, also in Shandong. Yang went on to introduce the system outside Shandong in Cangzhou, Hebei province. There he taught many students, most notably, Jia Yunhe, Liu Wenshi, Mi Lianke, Yang Kunshan, Liu Zhenshan, Jiang Rongjiao, and Lu Zhenduo, the late famous Mizong grandmaster (Lu, Qiu, & Wang, 1989: 1–2). Lu Zhenduo passed the system to his fourth child, Lu Junhai (the current 9th generation grandmaster and standard bearer of Qingping), who passed it to his first American disciple (as well as a small number of Chinese disciples), Hon K. Lee, who then taught the system to Reza Momenan, now a direct disciple of Lu. Lee and Momenan are passing it to just a handful of others (including the author of this article under Lee), while Lu recently began teaching the art to a few disciples in Great Britain.

Lu Zhengduo demonstrating
a Qingping application.

Principles of Qingping Sword Practice

From its earliest recorded history, the Qingping system was based on practical, tested knowledge of Chinese swordsmanship. The first published study on record about the Qingping sword discussed the "futility of mystifying the theories and exaggerating the capability of jian" use (Jiang, 1930: 13). The system trains in the use of the sixteen classical Chinese straight sword attributes: drop (*beng*), poke (*bo*), stab (*ci*), entangle (*chan*), copy (*chao*), point (*dian*), parry (*gua*), intercept (*jie*), obstruct (*lan*), glide-up (*liao*), press (*mo*), split (*pi*), raise (*ti*), slice-up (*tiao*), sweep (*shao*), circle (*yun*) (Fan, 2006). But it is distinct from other sword styles in how the routines that comprise the system are assembled.

Daoist in origin, Qingping swordsmanship is based on the concepts of Wudang sword arts. The Wudang method stresses finesse and containment of technique that responds in kind to the level of threat encountered.

> When using the jian, even in real fighting, you must never be hard or crude in your movements or your manner. Rather, you must use only high-level techniques and you must use them with subtlety and expertise. Your *yi* (mind) and *shen* (spirit), as well as your *qi* (intrinsic energy), must lead your movements and you must never show cruelty or ferocity. —Robinson, 2006b

Excellence in Qingping sword play is based on technical requirements that emphasize a methodology utilizing quick rises and falls, fast turns, and a combination of hardness and softness, imbued with broken, yet lucid rhythms. It relies on sophisticated footwork as the basis for handling the weapon and using it for combat. Attacks are often preceded by short, evasive steps going the opposite direction. Movements contain a high number of orthogonal actions in which the sword goes one way, while the body another way, and the legs yet another (Lee, 2002: 86).

Qingping sword's technical descriptors indicate the application of ancient martial concepts to the construct of this technically dense sword system. Throughout the more than 300 techniques that comprise the system, each possess a unique description. Technique names consists of four-character classical Chinese quotations. Chinese idiomatic names include "Brandishing Fan Against the Wind," "Sweeps Away Thousands of Enemy Forces," "Fair Lady Throws the Vase," "Search Plums in the Cloud," "Expansively Breaks the Plum Tree," "Purple Swallow Skims the Water," and "The Immortal Points the Right Way." All the terms have a unified pattern, integrating images and rationale that can be sung poetically. The system is especially noted for its varied content, which emphasize unpredictable attack and defense maneuvers "mixing truth and falsehood."

> The way of Qingping (swordsmanship) has a unique style. It is elegant and extraordinary. When in practice, it looks advancing but is in retreat. It is light and in transition. It is constantly changing. Sometimes, it is like passing cloud and flowing water. It stretches naturally and with poise. It suddenly attacks east and west. It abruptly sinks and floats as if it is the drifting duck weed. At times, it is like whipping wind and rushing cloud. It enforces with thunder-like violence and wind-like swiftness. It is as crazy as lightning and vigorous like a flying phoenix. Its routines and forms are of full content and rigorous structure. It incorporates force with grace. It mixes truth and falsehood. In offense, it has defense. In defense, it has offense. It has the rise and fall of masculinity and femininity and can appear and disappear mysteriously. —Lu, Qiu, & Wang, 1989: 3–4

Combining false moves with real attacks, Qingping sword utilizes postures and movements at the upper, middle, and lower plains, with most emphasis on lower plain ambushes, requiring a sophisticated ability to integrate internal and external power. The system was designed to cope with sudden changes, utilizing a tight structure, emphasizing delicacy, per the following.

- *Handling the straight sword.* Straight sword technique is focused on the wrist. The grasping of the sword handle must remain lively. It should not be held tightly so that it can coordinate with hand, eyes, body, method, and movements. The handling of the sword must be natural and spontaneous and achieves the state of oblivion. The positions of the wrist on the handle and the way the wrist holds the handle are different in various techniques. Thus, there is a saying that not to seal or block the enemy's attack and not to touch the enemy's weapon is the superior way of defeating the enemy. When the enemy attacks, we should intercept his wrist and then attack his body.

- *The waist must be in control—remaining light, flexible, vigorous, and nimble throughout.* The bodily movement in practicing Qingping jian relies entirely on the flexibility of the waist. It should achieve the integration of the body and sword. When the body turns the sword also turns. Advancing, retreating, dodging, extending, rising, lowering, and turning should all rely on the waist to guide the four limbs and overall skeletal structure, so that the force can be lively and smooth allowing strength to reach the tip of the sword. Once the bodily technique is achieved, hard and soft are combined, which exhibits both restraint and aggressiveness. That way, the complete spirit and power can be expressed.

Lu Junhai with Hon Lee, 2004. *Photos courtesy of Hon Lee.*

Qingping Sword Routines

The system is comprised of six solo routines and one two-person set. Each of the solo forms has over sixty movements, for a total of 365 movements, all poetically described in four-character verses around images of nature, Daoist concepts, and ancient sayings, with each technique corresponding to a single day of the year. The first form emphasizes an upright body and firm steps, with the five subsequent routines displaying rising, lowering, and turning movements.

Each form has its specially defined significance in actual combat. During combat, it takes the most succinct and quickest path; pays attention to the two or three inches of the wrist area, and realizes the special characteristics of defeating the enemy in short distance. In its methods, they have the moves of pursuing the enemy by a shortcut but also the way of defeating the enemy through evading being hit (or captured). They attack from a short distance in stretching the attack but also the method of tempting the enemy to come in deep into our own range in defeating him. The first move can set up an ambush for the next move. Thus, the second move can fulfill the effort of the first move. The sword is stretched out not knowing whether it is a true or false move. It aims to the left but attacks to the right. It attacks to the left but was aimed to the right. It uses surprise to defeat the enemy. —Qiu & Wang, 1984

Qingping and Chinese Sword Culture

The culture of swordsmanship revolves around the blade, the system, and the philosophy and skill of the warriors who wield them. In military culture, the sword represents an anchor of the warrior soul—a combative purity based on survival, technique, and the spirit required when using a blade in battle. Today, many cultures continue the tradition of swordsmanship as both a classical martial expression, as well as a combative technique. And while they still uphold ancient and sometimes secretive sword training, the prevalence of distinct, complete, systematic sword systems remain rare. But Chinese sword culture is especially acute in the idealization of sword arts as a virtue and an indication of one's social and cultural sophistication.

The jian is known as the 'gentleman's weapon', which means that if you practice the jian, you must do so with a sense of internal calm and correctness and that your movements must be beautiful. The jian is probably the most popular weapon in traditional Chinese martial arts because it is used in almost every style and is practiced by almost all groups. It is special because it is not just a martial arts weapon but also an important symbol to Chinese culture. It embodies the spirit of the Chinese people and has been celebrated in art and legend for thousands of years. It has come to express the most deeply held Chinese values and moral precepts. People practice jian not only to improve their health and fighting skills, but also to develop character and personality. —Robinson, 2006b

While such a view represents the romance of the sword, it does not speak to the significance the weapon holds as a preferred combat weapon of elite military professionals. As a refined warrior tool, mastery of the sword is considered essential to achieve the highest levels of martial art—levels that instill deadly skills requiring the utmost of moral character.

> Everything you do in your jian practice and in jian fighting should come from your heart, not just from your body. This is an attitude that has characterized jian forms for more than two thousand years and in this respect, the jian is different from any other martial arts weapon. For centuries, it has been a deeply held view in Chinese culture that the better your jian skills are, the finer your character must be. This traditional view holds that only people of superior character, such as heroes or other chivalrous individuals can truly use jian well. —Robinson, 2006b

Like most mature sword cultures, chivalry and warriorship intertwine around the ideals of swordsmanship in ancient China. In Chinese culture, knights and the swords they wielded underpinned both legend and reality. As such, the ideals linking present-day sword practice to the ancient spirit and knowledge of swordsmanship persist, despite the rarity of comprehensive Chinese sword arts. So while the ideals and philosophy of Chinese swordsmanship remain intact, the training methods and technique representing the highest standard of Chinese sword skill are not.

Chinese sword philosophy inspires, but does not offer practical guides to those seeking comprehensive Chinese sword mastery beyond the offerings of single forms embedded in martial art systems. Qingping jian, however, meshes the philosophical and technical ideals of swordsmanship from both legend and historical mentions extending from the Han dynasty. As perhaps the last surviving, stand-alone Chinese sword system, Qingping jian offers a rare practical guide on classical Chinese swordsmanship. The system's unique plethora of technique exhibits the ancient standards of Chinese swordsmanship systematically and without gaps. While the forms that comprise the system were likely constructed no earlier than the 1800s, Qingping jian's technical composition appear to be drawn from a much earlier history of Chinese sword knowledge.

The author practicing with the double-edge sword.
Photograph by Inbal More Photography.
www.inbalmore.com

INTERVIEW WITH LU JUNHAI

Conducted by Reza Momenan and Hon Lee

■ **Are the Qingping and Mizong systems related? It seems that some Qingping sword techniques are similar to Mizong techniques, e.g., body mechanics, footwork, etc.**

In principle, they are not at all related and are completely separate systems. Both are considered high level styles. Mizong boxing is of Buddhist origin and Qingping sword is of Daoist origin. Dragon-Tiger Mountain (*Long Hu Shan*) in Jiangxi Province is the birthplace of the Qingping system. Its creator was a Daoist priest named Pan Zhenren. His Daoist name was Yuan Kui. Many Daoist priests and Buddhist monks in ancient China were adept at martial arts because they had to know how to defend themselves during their travels as they ministered to the poor. During their travels they were often able to meet with other martial arts masters to exchange techniques and to gain new knowledge. Moreover, when martial artists see something good, they want to learn and make it their own. So it was with Pan, who pulled together all the best sword techniques that he had learned to create the Qingping sword system.

Cangzhou prefecture in Hebei province is the home of Mizong boxing. In Cangzhou there are many Mizong stylists who have studied the Qingping system. This sword art was brought to Cangzhou by a Daoist priest traveling though the area. [NB: Historical records indicate that the art was handed down to a Daoist priest named Jia Yunhe who resided in Cangzhou.] The locals, noticing the priest carried a sword across his back, invited him to stay so they could study with him. So it was with the people of Cangzhou who, upon recognizing that the traveling priest was a sword expert, wanted to learn Qingping sword from him. Whether the Qingping sword now practiced in Cangzhou was handed down to this traveling priest by Pan himself or from one of Pan's disciples is unclear. What is certain is that it is of Daoist origin.

■ **How did you learn the Qingping system? Did your father learn both the Mizong and Qingping systems from one person? Are there different versions and lineages? Which lineage is the standard?**

This sword art has been passed down from generation to generation in Cangzhou. I had learned both Mizong and Qingping from my father, a native of Cangzhou and my father had learned both arts from his teacher Yang Kunshan in Cangzhou. Because my father had studied both arts, one could say that, as far as our own lineage, each had influenced the other in terms of how techniques are performed. Those from other lineages will undoubtedly perform the same movements, but with characteristics that are unique to their own physiology, personality, and stylistic interpretations.

Furthermore, there are different Qingping lineages. It is said that the traveling priest who first brought the art to Cangzhou initially resided on the western side of the Yun River that divided the area. He taught the people of western Cangzhou four out of the six sets of Qingping sword. However, he felt that the people there were too boastful, so he moved to the eastern side of the river where he taught six sets. The people of the western side snuck over to observe the eastern side. There, they stole the secrets of the remaining sets. According to the story, the easterners learned all six sets directly from the priest, while the westerners learned the last two only by observation from a distance. So it is said that the easterners knowledge was the most complete.

There are also differences and variations of Qingping sword even within the same lineage. For example, if a disciple is talented he might learn the teacher's moves well and pass them on correctly. But if the disciple was not good, that is a different matter. There may be those who claim that their version of Qingping sword is the most accurate, but I would never make such a statement or to criticize anyone's version. All I can say is, "I learned from my father. This is my version of Qingping sword."

■ **So, as to why we see similar movements in Mizong and Qingping, you are saying that it is the result of how you and your father do them based on what you bring the performance as individual martial artists?**

Yes, I use the body mechanics that I have developed from Mizong to express the art of Qingping and vice versa, just as my father did. Students of other martial arts, for example bagua, will perform Qingping with a flavor or unique style that is influenced by their art. This is a natural and easily understandable phenomenon that occurs whether you're talking about Qingping or some other weapon or empty hand form. For example, let's say that we teach two people the staff. Take a practitioner of Northern Shaolin and a practitioner of Southern Shaolin. Teach them the same staff form, same moves, same steps, but it will definitely come out looking entirely different. They in turn teach their students. Can you say which one should be considered the standard? That's why I would never make the claim that what I do should be called the correct version.

■ **Are there only six Qingping sets? If so, what are the main features of the six?**

The first routine is foundation set. If you learn the 1st, well, then you can learn the others more easily. The first routine, *di yi lu*, is like the fundamental Spring

Leg (*Tantui*) training in the Mizong system. It should not be performed quickly and provides the fundamentals needed for the other sets. Even before attempting it, however, you must have good basics and should have developed a solid foundation in boxing or barehanded forms (*quanshu*) before attempting to learn the Qingping sword.

The first routine emphasizes more stable stances and correct footwork. Body movements and sword technique changes are slower than in the other remaining sets. You must completely understand the basic techniques embodied in "sixteen words" when performing the sets as well as the applications of each move. For example, you have to understand how, when, and why you execute the sixteen fundamental straight sword techniques. Once you can do these sixteen basic techniques accurately and can understand the principles behind them that are contained in the first routine correctly, then you won't have problems performing the other five routines.

As you progress through the six routines, the moves become more fluid and lively, with directional changes and sword techniques more complex and rapid. In routines number five and six, the special characteristics are essentially the same. Qingping sword techniques places great emphasis on movements that are nimble, fluid and graceful. While each of the six sets are supposed to contain certain special characteristics, their explanations have been lost over time. Many martial arts experts, unfortunately, were illiterate and were unable to pass on their knowledge in written form.

■ **What differentiates Qingping from other well-known Chinese sword routines? Why is it considered the "crown jewel" of Chinese swordsmanship when other famous routines also focus on techniques that are also to be nimble, fluid and graceful?**

I personally believe that over time people who are knowledgeable about traditional Chinese swordsmanship have been able to make side-by-side comparisons of the Qingping sword system with other similar sword systems and have judged that it is better able to express the sixteen basic techniques in a way that is more dynamic, fluid and graceful. Moreover, it has a unique style all its own and very different from the rest. But, of course, the person performing Qingping must be able to bring out these qualities, otherwise it's just empty talk.

■ **Is Qingping famous because it's beautiful to watch because of these qualities, or because it can be used for fighting? Which made it more famous?**

Both! These qualities certainly make it beautiful to watch, but it's fluid and dynamic techniques are practical and can be used for combat. Some martial arts are "flowery hands, embroidered legs," meaning that they are nice to look at, but have no practical application. The special qualities expressed in Qingping sword movement are the very same ones that can be used for fighting.

■ **Why are there six Qingping sets? Are they complete?**

Of all the well-known sword methods, the Qingping sword is the longest and has the most movements and techniques. There are 365 separate techniques. If you learn one technique a day, it would take you one year to learn the whole thing.

Daoist priest Pan must have been a highly educated person because he was able to use a four-character phrase to describe each of the 365 techniques, with almost no repetition in the phrases. These four-character phrases are common sayings (*cheng yu*) that are often references to something in Chinese literature or history or a well-known story. Moreover, the phrases evoke images that closely match the sword movements.

■ **Can the Qingping system be taught to anyone or should they have certain qualifications?**

Let's look at this from two angles. First, the potential Qingping sword student should have the ability to learn it well, which means first of all that the student should be good with empty hand methods. If his empty hand practice is poor, he will never learn the sword well.

■ **Let's say that someone wants to learn Qingping sword, has an excellent martial arts background, but not in Mizong. Can he or she be taught, provided they are of good moral character?**

Yes, not only can you teach them if they have the necessary foundation and have good moral character, you should teach them. Having them start with Spring Leg training (*Tantui*) when they already have a solid base to learn Qingping would not be reasonable. However, sometimes it's harder to discern whether they have the right martial ethics than assessing their martial skills. For example, a student whom I thought was a good person started teaching others without my permission after only studying with me for a year. Because he lacked martial morality, I asked him not to come back even though he apologized to me and wanted to turn his students over to me.

■ **Are the six sets of Qingping complete or are some lost?**

It's a complete system as far as what I've inherited from his father, and is the one I'm passing on to my disciples.

DESCRIPTIONS: Six Solo Routines and One Two-Person Set

Routine 1: The first Qingping sword routine trains the basics of point, drop, and stab. These three technical attributes form the foundation of Qingping sword practice. Poetically described, the important techniques of "dragonfly dips into water," and "golden cock nods its head," stress the use of point. The "poisonous scorpion turns its tail" and "the fairy points the way" emphasize drop, while the "golden flower drops to the ground" and "beautiful maiden throws the vase" trains stab (Qiu & Wang, 1984). With an emphasis on symmetry and sword handling, the movements (footwork and body motions) are symmetrical and linear in execution. The routine executes techniques in sequence of the hand following the feet, and the feet following the body.

Routine 2: The moves are light and floating so as to engage a fleeting, hard to catch target with intense, penetrating thrusts (Qiu & Wang, 1984). The techniques deviate from symmetric coordination to non-linear techniques, moving the body parts around different axes. Among those are frequent direction changes executed at a faster pace, with aerial (skipping and leaping) techniques.

Routine 3: The body mechanics sometimes pulls in and sometimes pushes out with contracting and expanding movements/energies. The movements are controlled, yet extremely lively, with very natural body twists and turns. Defense against multiple attackers is introduced with an emphasis on constant direction and targeting changes, building intermediate level skill. The flexibility and flare of the movements are reminiscent of Tang Dynasty (618–907 CE) ideals, China's renaissance period when poetry and the arts were in full bloom (Qiu & Wang, 1984).

Routine 4: The movements are tightly linked together as a shield against other attacks. The movements are varied and unpredictable, and emerge from a compact structure with the swordsman adhering strictly to the rules of system. The upper body guides the footwork, requiring a more sophisticated connection between the upper and lower body. Techniques are now expressed with the body following the feet, and the feet following the hands. The techniques become more circular requiring more skill in targeting, while exhibiting more overt focused power issuing (*jing*).

Routine 5: This routine emphasizes highly complex evasive and deceptive techniques, including sudden high-low or low-high movements, including techniques where the weapon changes hands. Switching the hands holding the sword is like shooting an arrow first to the right and then to left: transforming in a completely new direction to take the enemy by surprise (Qiu & Wang, 1984).

Routine 6: More offensive, one's attention penetrates to the left and right with techniques that combine advancing with retreating in movement (Qiu & Wang, 1984). This final set requires mastery of the foregoing routines, with movements executed in eight directions in a constantly changing order of the body and limbs sequence, where the leading of the body, feet, and hands constantly changes, requiring the highest levels of coordination and control.

Partner Form: The two-person routine teaches applications at close and long range, emphasizing the foregoing requirements with an emphasis on footwork, wrist targeting, evasiveness, and smooth sword contact with directional and tempo changes.

QINGPING SWORD APPLICATIONS GUIDE

Application #1: The following selection from the third routine illustrates upper and lower limb attacks.

- Oriole Captures Bramble Finch (*ying pu yen que*)
- Canary Blackens Its Eyebrows (*jin shi hua mei*)
- Step Forward and Lift Knee (*jin bu ti xi*)
- Change Location, Mythical Dragon Rises (*yi di qi jiao*)

(1) Lu Junhai deflects Reza Momenan's lower right stab, (2) redirecting upward into an upper right stab to Momenan's neck. Momenan defends (3), lifting his left leg, attacking to the upper right. Lu evades (4), lifting his left leg, while attacking Momenan's right wrist. Momenan steps with the left leg, for a lower attack, which Lu evades (5), stepping back with the left. He lifts his right leg attacking downward to slice the outside of Momenan's right wrist. *Photos courtesy of Hon Lee.*

Application #2: Qingping's use of hand-switching is introduced in the Fifth Routine. Series A shows form; series B shows application.

• Turn Yin and Yang Upside Down (*dian dao yin yang*)

Momenan attacks Lu with a low stab. Lu defends, lifting his left leg, flicking his sword downward to Momenan's wrist (1). Momenan then attacks high (2). Lu responds by cross-stepping with the right leg, slicing to Momenan's outer right wrist (3). Momenan steps around Lu with the left leg, attacking low (4). Lu blocks and Momenan attacks high. Lu then employs side cross stepping (5), passing his sword from the right to the left hand moving into closer range, slicing Momenan's right inner forearm.

TABLE "Sixteen Words"

Qingping sword routines train the practitioner in sixteen classical Chinese straight sword techniques. The technical methodology of these sword techniques are concisely described by Lu Junhai as the "sixteen words" of the system. One or more moves comprise a technique. For example, the technique "immortal draws map" in routine #1 consists of three movements: high sweep, reverse parry, and reverse thrust. Unless otherwise noted in the following, techniques are offensive.

點 1) Chinese: *Dian*
Action: flick tip down
Mechanics: arm straight, index grip, sudden force to tip
Sample Technique: Phoenix Nods Head

English: point, touch
Target: wrist, forearm

繃 2) Chinese: *Beng*
Action: flick tip up or in arm
Mechanics: straight, hammer grip, sudden snap up or in
Sample Technique: Poison Scorpion Flips Tail

English: tighten, bounce
Target: wrist, throat

刺 3) Chinese: *Ci*
Action: straight pierce
Mechanics: arm straight, index grip, palm in/out/or down
Sample Technique: Golden Compass Needle

English: thrust, stab
Target: head, body, legs

撩 4) Chinese: *Liao*
Action: slice or cut upward
Mechanics: palm left or right, index grip, force at blade front
Sample Technique: Daoist Priest Brushes Dust

English: glide up
Target: wrist, forearm

撩 5) Chinese: *Pi*
Action: chop w/shoulder force
Mechanics: index or hammer grip, palm left or right
Sample Technique: Split Mt. Hua Forcefully

English: split, chop
Target: head, neck, body

掛 6) Chinese: *Gua*
Action: circles down and back
Mechanics: hammer grip, palm left or right, use flat of blade
Sample Technique: Fisherman Asks for Ferry

English: circular parry
Target: defense

纏　7) Chinese: *Chan*　　　　　　　　　　English: coil, entangle
　　Action: tip encircles wrist　　　　　　　Target: seek opening
　　Mechanics: index grip, palm down or left, wrist/elbow/shoulder
　　Sample Technique: (in routine 2)

截　8) Chinese: *Jie*　　　　　　　　　　　English: intercept, stop
　　Action: block and dodge, saw　　　　　Target: forearm
　　Mechanics: hammer grip, block and counter with sawing motion
　　Sample Technique: (in routine 6)

提　9) Chinese: *Ti*　　　　　　　　　　　English: raise, lift
　　Action: evade and cut upward　　　　　Target: forearm
　　Mechanics: hammer grip, cut as sword is raised overhead
　　Sample Technique: Wave Fan Against Wind

抄　10) Chinese: *Chao*　　　　　　　　　English: seize circular
　　Action: scoop and stick　　　　　　　　Target: defense
　　Mechanics: hammer grip, scoop up, guide and stick to weapon
　　Sample Technique: (in routine 3)

掃　11) Chinese: *Sao*　　　　　　　　　　English: sweep horizontal
　　Action: slice　　　　　　　　　　　　　Target: various
　　Mechanics: index grip, arm & shoulder, high, middle or low
　　Sample Technique: Part Grass Find Snake

雲　12) Chinese: *Yun*　　　　　　　　　　English: cloud circle
　　Action: circle blade overhead　　　　　Target: defense
　　Mechanics: loose grip, horizontal circle overhead, tilt head back
　　Sample Technique: Goose Rouses Feathers

欄　13) Chinese: *Lan*　　　　　　　　　　English: obstruct, block
　　Action: push against weapon　　　　　　Target: weapon, forearm
　　Mechanics: hammer grip, blade center pushes away or attacks
　　Sample Technique: Jade Lady Presents Book

撥　14) Chinese: *Bo*　　　　　　　　　　　English: poke aside
　　Action: flick outward, palm up　　　　　Target: head, body, arms
　　Mechanics: loose then hammer grip, sudden force to tip
　　Sample Technique: Part Clouds Watch Sun

挑 15) Chinese: *Tiao*   English: pick-upward

Action: swing upward   Target: chest, throat

Mechanics: hammer grip, swing back or forward, use shoulder

Sample Technique: Immortal Shows Way

抹 16) Chinese: *Mo*   English: wipe, smear

Action: horizontal swiping   Target: head, chest

Mechanics: hammer grip, palm down, swiping left or right

Sample Technique: (in routine 2)

Bibliography

Fan, Xiao (2006). *Qingping jian* (Internet), National Yunlin University of Science and Technology, http://www.ee.yuntech.edu.tw/~htchang/teach_12.htm, Taiwan.

Lee, Hon K. (August 2002). The rare art of Qingping jian (Green Water Lily sword), *Kung Fu Tai Chi*.

Li, Meibin (November 1984). Wushu: Nationwide Systemization, *China Sports*.

Lu, Junhai; Qiu, Pixiang; and Wang, Peikun (1989). *Qingping Jian Shu, Lu 1–6*. Beijing: Renmin Tiyu Chuban She (Peoples Sports Publishing House).

Jiang, Rongqiao (Ed.) (January 1930). *Xie Zheng Qingping Jian* (*Portraying the Qingping Sword*). Part of the Wu Bei Cong Shu (Books on Armaments) series edited by the Shanghai Militaristic and Virtue Improvement Association, Shanghai World Book Publishing.

Jones, R. (October 2005). *Tai Chi notes blog* (Internet). http://realtaichi.blogspot.com/2005/10/traditional-chinese-sword-culture.html

Kennedy, B. (May 2007). *Martial talk–Sword talk forum* (Internet). http://www.martial-talk.com/forum/showthread.php?p=797455.

Kennedy, B. and Guo, E. (2005). *Martial arts training manuals: A historical survey*. Berkeley: North Atlantic Books.

Momenan, Reza and Lee, Hon K. (September 4, 2006). Lu Junhai interview. London.

Qiu, Pixiang (November 1984). An ancient routine rejuvenated. *China Sports*.

Qiu, Pixiang and Wang, Peikun (1984). *Qingping Jian* (VHS). Shanghai Tiyu Xue Yuan (Shanghai Physical Culture Institute). Qiu and Wang shot the film with support from the Shanghai Physical Culture Institute, Teaching and Research Office and Electronic Education.

Robinson, L. (2006). "History of straight sword (jian) in China" (Internet), Master Forge Limited. http://www.masterforge.co.uk/acatalog/Traditional-hand-forged-Chinese-Jian-swords.html.

Robinson, L. (2006). "The jian (straight sword) in Chinese culture" (Internet), Master Forge Limited. http://www.masterforge.co.uk/acatalog/Traditional-hand-forged-Chinese-Jian-swords.html.

Tom, P. (1998). "The art of the Chinese sword" (Internet). Seven Stars Trading Co. http://www.sevenstarstrading.com/articles/articles.php?subpage=art

index

Made in the USA
Coppell, TX
08 April 2023

15409609R00046